CW00556495

CONTENTS

The Transport Treasury

D206 at KINGS CROSS • From October 1958, the brand new English Electric Type 4 1Co-Co1 2000hp locomotives were put in charge of some of the most prestigious East coast Main Line services including *The Flying Scotsman*. A task they would share with their steam forefathers for several more years. D206 entered service in July 1958 at Hornsey depot (34B) and performed well for 25 years before being withdrawn in March 1983. Generations of steam locomotives have certainly left their soot-encrusted footprint on Kings Cross signal box. The locomotive waits for the signal before performing the once familiar zig-zag manoeuvre into Gasworks Tunnel, then back into the headshunt for the loco sidings. Fortunately, out of the 200 class members, seven escaped the cutters torch and we can still enjoy the sights and sounds of these beasts, but rarely at this station. *Photo: D. Brennand Collection*

INTRODUCTION

A warm welcome to the first issue of Eastern Times from Transport Treasury Publishing, we hope that you enjoy the content in this periodical.

We aim to bring you differing and interesting articles from the LNER, the many railway companies that preceded the formation of the LNER in 1923 and similarly the successor to the LNER when the company was divided into the new British Railways' Eastern Region, North Eastern Region and part of the Scottish Region.

A vast area was covered, stretching north and east from London to Edinburgh on the way taking in the cities of York and Newcastle-upon-Tyne in England with Aberdeen and Inverness being served on the journey north from the Scottish capital. The LNER even ventured to the western-most point of the railway network in Scotland, over to Liverpool by its joint ownership of the Cheshire Lines Committee and to Wrexham in North Wales courtesy of the Great Central Railway.

A number of the country's coalfields, shipyards and docks were also served by the railway, lines being constructed into the industrial areas of the North East and Humberside and to the holiday resorts of Lincolnshire and East Anglia.

We start this new series with articles on the West Highland Extension, Humberside and Lincolnshire and a royal visit to Stratford Depot by the late Queen Elizabeth II, all accompanied by fabulous photography from The Transport Treasury archives. Most of the images are available to purchase in differing formats, hence if you see something you would like for your collection, please don't hesitate to contact us; details can be found on the inside front cover.

We want to involve the reader in this series so if you see anything that may be erroneous. please let us know, and indeed, if you have any suggestions or feel as though you have some interesting material to share with us don't hesitate to send in your contributions.

PETER SIKES, EDITOR, EASTERN TIMES
email: tteasterntimes@gmail.com

Front cover (and inset right): Durham is the location as world-record speed holder No. 60022 *Mallard* enters the station with a southbound express.

LNER CONSTITUENT COMPANIES

THE FOLLOWING MADE UP THE LONDON AND NORTH EASTERN RAILWAY AS A RESULT OF THE RAILWAYS ACT 1921:

CONSTITUENT COMPANIES		
Railway Company	Route miles/km	Notes
Great Eastern Railway (GER)	1,191¼ miles (1,906km)	
Great Central Railway (GCR)	852½ miles (1,364km)	
Great Northern Railway (GNR)	1,051¼ miles (1,680km)	
Great North of Scotland Railway (GNSR)	334½ miles (535km)	
Hull and Barnsley Railway (H&BR)	106½ miles (170km)	Amalgamated with the NER on 1 April 1922
North British Railway (NBR)	1,378 miles (2,218km)	
North Eastern Railway (NER)	1,757¾ miles (2,812km)	

SUBSIDIARY COMPANIES Independently operated lines		
Railway Company	**Route miles/km**	**Notes**
Colne Valley and Halstead Railway	19 miles (31km)	
East and West Yorkshire Union Railway	9½ miles (15km)	
Mid-Suffolk Light Railway	19½ miles (31km)	
LEASED OR WORKED RAILWAYS Some existed only in name and were included at the time of the Railways Act in order to legally qualify each line's position		
Brackenhill Light Railway (West Yorkshire)		Leased to or worked by the NER
East Lincolnshire Railway	47½ miles (76km)	Leased to or worked by the GNR
Edinburgh and Bathgate Railway	10¼ miles (16km)	Leased to or worked by the NBR
Fawcett Depot line (County Durham)	5½ miles (9km)	Leased to or worked by the NER
Forth and Clyde Junction Railway	30½ miles (49km)	Leased to or worked by the NBR
Gifford & Garvald Railway	9¼ miles (15km)	Leased to or worked by the NBR
Glasgow and Milngavie Junction Railway	3¼ miles (5km)	Leased to or worked by the NBR and worked jointly with Caledonian Railway
Great North of England, Clarence and Hartlepool Junction line	8½ miles (13.5km)	Leased to or worked by the NER
Horncastle Railway	7½ miles (12km)	Leased to or worked by the GNR
Humber Commercial Railway and Dock		Leased to or worked by the GCR
Lauder Light Railway	10¼ miles (16km)	Leased to or worked by the NBR
London and Blackwall Railway	6 miles (9.7km)	Leased to or worked by the GER
Mansfield Railway	10 miles (16km)	Leased to or worked by the GCR
Newburgh and North Fife Railway	13¼ miles (21km)	Leased to or worked by the NBR
North Lindsey Light Railway	12 miles (19km)	Leased to or worked by the GCR
Nottingham and Grantham Railway and Canal	23 miles (37km)	Leased to or worked by the GNR
Nottingham Joint Station Committee		Leased to or worked by several constituent companies
Nottingham Suburban line	4 miles (6.4km)	Leased to or worked by the GNR
Seaforth and Sefton Junction Railway		Leased to or worked by the GCR
Sheffield District Railway	4½ miles (7km)	Leased to or worked by the GCR
South Yorkshire Junction Railway	11½ miles (18km)	Originally leased to or worked by H&BR
Stamford and Essendine Railway	12½ miles (20km)	Leased to or worked by the GNR
West Riding and Grimsby Railway	32½ miles (52km)	Leased to or worked by several constituent companies

Left: Metro-Cammell units cross at a very snowy Castleton Moor station on the Esk Valley line with Whitby Town and Middlesbrough services. Situated in the heart of the lovely North Yorkshire countryside, the station was once terminus of the line from Picton on the Yarm to Northallerton route before the NER completed the section to Grosmont. *Photo: © Transport Treasury*

INDEPENDENTLY OPERATED JOINT COMPANIES		
Railway Company	Route miles/km	Notes
Cheshire Lines Committee (CLC)		Operated jointly by LNER/London, Midland and Scottish Railway (LMS). LNER supplies locomotive power; CLC own rolling stock.
East London Railway (ELR)		Jointly leased by the LNER, Southern Railway, Metropolitan Railway (MetR) and District Railway. Traffic operated by MetR (passenger); LNER (goods).
Manchester, South Junction and Altrincham Railway		Trains worked by both LNER/LMSR
JOINT RAILWAYS After 1923 part of London & North Eastern Railway		
Great Northern and Great Eastern Joint Railway	123 miles (198km)	
Hull and Barnsley and Great Central Joint Railway	25¾ miles (41.4km)	
JOINT RAILWAYS with London, Midland & Scottish Railway		
Axholme Joint Railway	27+3⁄4 miles (44.7km)	
Cheshire Lines Committee	142 miles (229km)	Two-thirds share
Caledonian and Dunbartonshire Junction Railway	7 miles (11km)	Including Loch Lomond steamers
Dundee and Arbroath Railway	23 miles (37km)	Including Carmyllie Light Railway
Great Central and Midland Joint Railway	40¼ miles (64.8km)	
Great Central & North Staffordshire Joint Railway	11 miles (18km)	
Great Northern and London and North Western Joint Railway	45 miles (72km)	
Halifax and Ovenden Junction Railway	2½ miles (4.0km)	
Methley Railway	6 miles (9.7km)	Two-thirds share
Midland and Great Northern Joint Railway	183¼ miles (294.9km)	
Norfolk and Suffolk Joint Railway	22¼ miles (35.8km)	Three-quarters share
Oldham, Ashton and Guide Bridge Railway	6¼ miles (10.1km)	
Otley & Ilkley Railway	6¼ miles (10.1km)	
Perth General Station		Two-thirds share
Prince's Dock, Glasgow	1¼ miles (2.0km)	One-third share
South Yorkshire Joint Railway	20½ miles (33.0km)	Three-fifths share
Swinton and Knottingley Joint Railway	19½ miles (31.4km)	
Tottenham & Hampstead Junction Railway	4¾ miles (7.6km)	
JOINT RAILWAYS with Great Western Railway		
Great Western and Great Central Joint Railway	41 miles (66km)	

LOWESTOFT SENTINEL

A pose for the camera from the footplate of Civil Engineer's Departmental Locomotive No. 38 as it pauses in between duties at Lowestoft Civil Engineer's Depot sometime in 1954.

Sentinel LNER Class Y3 0-4-0VBT No. 38 was built in September 1930 by Sentinel Waggon Works and entered service for the LNER as No. 61, being renumbered in September 1946 to No. 8168. Although allocated a BR number this was not applied and in March 1953 it was entered into BR Departmental Stock as No. 38 until withdrawal in February 1959.

Photo: A.W.V. Mace © Transport Treasury

THE WEST HIGHLAND RAILWAY MALLAIG EXTENSION

BY IAN LAMB

My father promised me that when I was ten years old he would take me on the greatest railway journey in the world – 'The West Highland' line – and I was not disappointed. However (appreciating the scenery apart), the railway was built to capture the vast fishing trade that lay in the hidden depths of the Sound of Sleat and the seas beyond.

There are many ways of seeing landscape, and none more vivid, in spite of canting dilettanti, than from a railway train.

Robert Louis Stevenson

According to John Thomas, "The West Highland was a railway within a railway. It had its own board of directors and its own capital (later it was to have its own very special atmosphere), but the North British had undertaken to staff and work the line with its own men, engines and rolling stock." The Mallaig extension received Royal Assent on 31st July 1894, and opened to the public on 1st April 1901.

In March 1892, a Government committee picked Mallaig Bay as the best place for a railway terminus. They suggested that a breakwater be built to enclose thirty acres of water and a railway be constructed to connect with the existing 'NBR' line at Banavie, not far from Fort William.

Circa 1985/86 • Slowly making its way at the compulsory 20mph across the classic Glenfinnan viaduct beneath the slopes of the mighty Beinn an Tuim (810m), a Class 37 locomotive and its train head east with probably the early afternoon service direct from Mallaig to Glasgow (Queen Street), reversing at Fort William. *Photo: Graham Smith*

A view of Mallaig Pier from a departing ferry. On the left of the picture we see a rake of fish vans waiting to be loaded before heading south for Billingsgate. © *Transport Treasury*

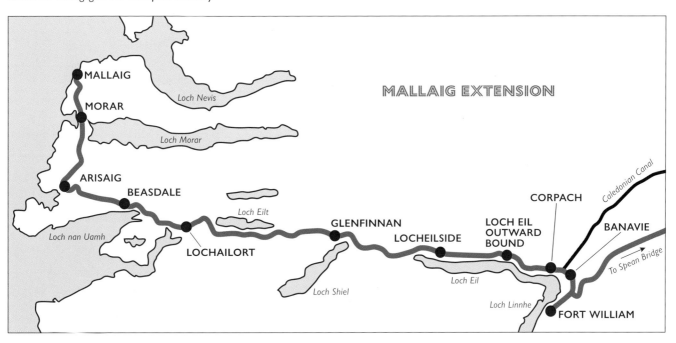

31st July 1956 • Gresley K1 Class 2-6-0 No. 62052 waits for the signal to depart Mallaig.
Photo: A. E. Bennett © Transport Treasury

The engineers were Simpson & Wilson, and the contractors were Robert McAlpine & Sons, both from Glasgow. It had always been difficult to operate this route, due to weight restrictions and sharp curves, problems that tested successive railway locomotive designers.

As a young engineering apprentice during the late 1950s, I was placed on a week's outdoor course in the West Highlands. With some trepidation I joined my fellow apprentices outside the factory, and boarded a very old ex-wartime short wheel based jeep for an overnight journey. The roads north were very basic in those days, and the vehicle's seats so hard that I'm sure my backside was red raw by the time we reached Glenfinnan!

On the early morning of Saturday 2nd July 1960 we arrived at the shores of Loch Shiel and I was simply mesmerised with the natural beauty of the overall scene. The Jacobite Monument stood sentinel as the dawn arrived, backed by the incredible outline of the railway viaduct. However, my main concern of the moment was looking at the rather fragile canvas double canoes which we were instructed to load up and pack ourselves into the very small cockpits. I was terrified; but I just loved outdoor adventure. This may be the beginning of the outdoor experience, but I was more worried about its end because I had purchased

October 1964 • Two views of Mallaig engine shed with all track lifted. As can be seen it comprised a single road and was located on the west side of the station by the sea. It was approached from the south and the facilities included a turntable, a line to the east of the shed extended to the pier. The shed survived for some time after the turntable was removed and track lifted, seeing various usage including the storage of fish boxes. It was demolished in 1987. *Photo above: P. J. Rowe. Photo below: Norris Forrest © Transport Treasury*

21st July 1958 • Beavertail observation car No. E1719E pictured at Mallaig station at the rear of the 2.45pm to Glasgow Queen Street via Fort William. The carriage was preserved and is now in the care of Railway Vehicle Preservations (RVP), being located at the Great Central Railway in Leicestershire. *Photo: W.A.C. Smith © Transport Treasury*

21st July 1958 • Class K1 2-6-0 No. 62012 shunting at Mallaig when the terminus possessed platform canopies. Regrettably these were removed some twenty years later. *Photo: W.A.C. Smith © Transport Treasury*

MALLAIG EXTENSION GRADIENT PROFILE

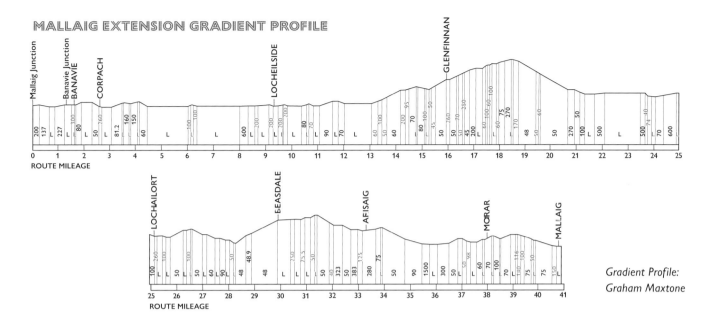

Gradient Profile: Graham Maxtone

a week's "Freedom of Scotland" railway ticket with the intention of exploring as many of the lines as possible which were destined for closure under the 'Beeching Act'.

Nevertheless, I was concerned that I might miss the early morning train south from Mallaig, so when the last service of Friday 8th July 1960 came in from Fort William, the duty station master kindly 'locked' me in the train to ensure there was no way in which I would be late. The compartment coaches in these days enabled one to have a long stretch out in 'sofa' comfort, especially after a week on the hard camping grounds of remote Scotland!

Thompson K1 engine No. 62052 (65J) allocated, had 63B on the firebox door, indicating the various codes under which Fort William shed had been registered.

06.30 MALLAIG–FORT WILLIAM K1 CLASS 2-6-0 No. 62052	
Mallaig (depart)	06.30
Morar	–
Arisaig	–
Lochailort	–
Glenfinnan	07.28
Locheilside	–
Corpach	07.52
Banavie	07.56
Fort William (arrive)	08.02

We left Mallaig on time and headed up the 1 in 50 gradient from the end of the level platform. There was a three minute delay at Mallaig signal box to uplift the single-line tablet. Just beyond the outskirts of this small fishing town the railway descends at varying inclines to almost level at Morar.

Morar level crossing and station looking west. *Photo: Norris Forrest*

Speed averaged 40mph between Morar and Arisaig. The single-line tablets were exchanged at Arisaig whilst the train was in motion. Now running down a 1 in 350 incline to Mains of Arisaig before levelling out to Coille Ropach, then descending again at 1 in 50 towards Loch nan Uamh, glistening with the morning dew.

Loch Dubh appeared like a millpond as the train levelled out and curved sharply above the narrow Loch Ailort before crawling into the station. Again tablets were exchanged whilst in transit – quite an admirable skill by the railwaymen concerned.

The surface on Loch Eilt was quite rough, surprisingly for such a small expanse of water. Now the beat of the engine changed in approaching the long and steep incline, whilst the surrounding hills flung back the echoes of the K1's roar as its thundering staccato reverberated from the track to the summit above Glenfinnan.

Now downhill on a 1 in 50 incline the train coasted at the maximum allowed speed of 20mph onto the magnificent curved 21-arch concrete viaduct straddling the historic amphitheatre above the spectacular Loch Shiel. The reflections on the loch's dark and still waters were fantastic against the light green of the mountains.

For the moment my heart was pounding as I recalled my anxiety a week earlier setting off with a certain amount of fear in a rather fragile-looking canvas canoe from the inlet far below. The tall, slender '45 monument served as a pointer 'downloch' where the darkened clouds reflected on the surface beneath the morning sun. Out of sight in the far distance was the open sea where I thought I'd never survive, and for the moment I could still feel the waves crashing over us whilst the salt spray stung our eyes.

Beyond the Glenfinnan defile, the sea at Loch Eil was calm and peaceful where the railway runs level at its side. The train averaged 45mph down the 1 in 200 incline on the approach to Locheilside station. Lupins were in full bloom and rowan trees threaded the side of the loch. To all intents and purposes the train coasted into Corpach station on time clattering over the Caledonian Canal swing-bridge. Running on the level into Fort William was no problem for 62052 as it steamed its train into the station where it was uniquely placed on the shores of Loch Linnhe.

Although former Stanier LMS designed 'Black Five' engines gradually encroached onto the West Highland line, it was Gresley's K2s that dominated the Mallaig extension. The latter were a Great Northern Railway design dating back to 1914, and chiefly intended for freight work. Following the 'railway grouping' of 1923 fourteen K2 machines were transferred to Scotland in 1925, initially to cope with the increasing weight of trains over the mountainous terrain. They were joined by a further six in 1932, reaching a total of thirty by 1951. Conversions to the cab were made (including side windows) to give some comfort to the locomotive crew from the notoriously inclement Scottish weather, and thirteen received names of West Highland lochs. By 1961 only *Loch Arkaig* remained in service and W. A. C. Smith – who organised many special excursions – arranged for that engine to make a farewell trip to Crianlarich in June of that year.

21st July 1958 • Gresley GNR Class K2 mogul No. 61784 takes water at Glenfinnan station with the 2.45pm train from Mallaig to Fort William and Glasgow. *Photo: W.A.C. Smith © Transport Treasury*

Class K1 locomotives Nos. 62031 and 62012 pictured at Arisaig, head the 5.45am from Glasgow (Queen Street) to Mallaig. It may seem incongruous that the furthest west station in Britain was once the preserve of the LNER. *Photo: W.A.C. Smith © Transport Treasury*

Thompson Class B1 4-6-0 No. 61342 pictured arriving at Banavie station with a Mallaig service.
Photo: Norris Forrest © Transport Treasury

A view of Mallaig Junction (now named Fort William Junction) looking west. *Photo: Norris Forrest © Transport Treasury*

18th July 1955 • Class K2/2 2-6-0 No. 61775 arrives at Fort William with the 2.45pm from Mallaig.
Photo: W.A.C. Smith © Transport Treasury

5th September 1954 • Class K2 2-6-0 No. 61764 *Loch Arkaig* rests quietly at Fort William motive power depot.
Photo: W.A.C. Smith © Transport Treasury

5th September 1954 • Class J36 0-6-0s Nos. 65300 and 65313 at Fort William shed together with 'Black Five' No. 44921.
Photo: W.A.C. Smith © Transport Treasury

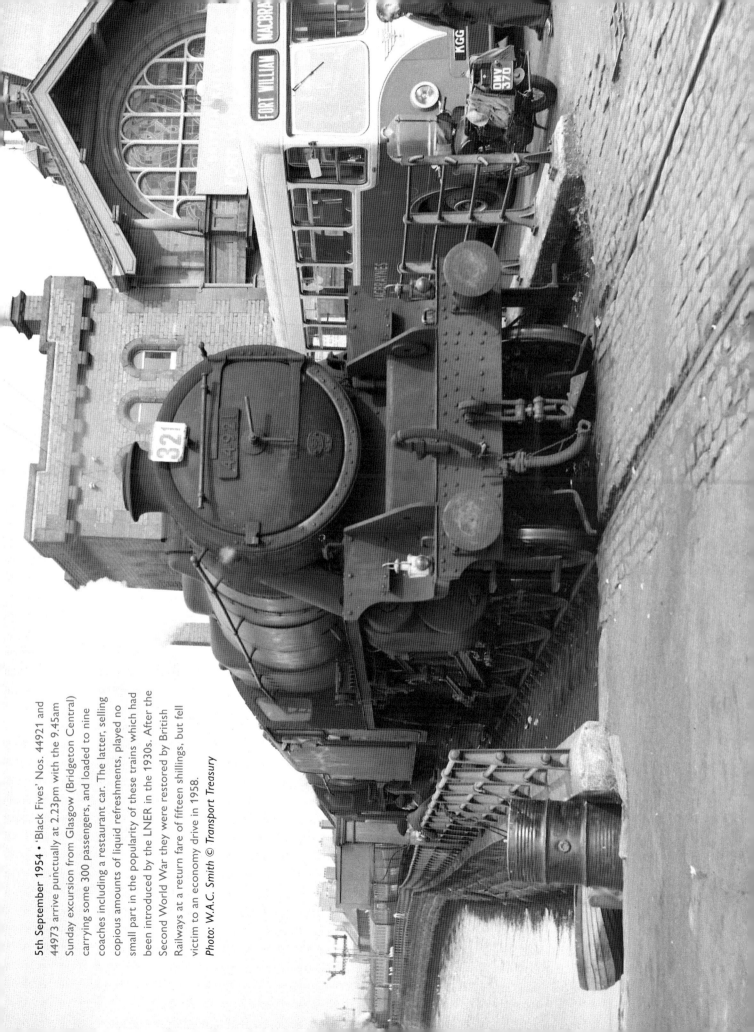

5th September 1954 • 'Black Fives' Nos. 44921 and 44973 arrive punctually at 2.23pm with the 9.45am Sunday excursion from Glasgow (Bridgeton Central) carrying some 300 passengers, and loaded to nine coaches including a restaurant car. The latter, selling copious amounts of liquid refreshments, played no small part in the popularity of these trains which had been introduced by the LNER in the 1930s. After the Second World War they were restored by British Railways at a return fare of fifteen shillings, but fell victim to an economy drive in 1958.

Photo: W.A.C. Smith © Transport Treasury

Two views of Reid-designed North British 'Glen' Class D34 4-4-0 No. 62477 *Glen Dochart* pictured shortly after arrival at Fort William station and, below, taking on coal at Fort William shed. *Photos: Sandy Murdoch*

18th June 1960 • Veteran Holmes Class J36 0-6-0 No. 65313,
built by the North British Railway at Cowlairs in 1899,
shunts empty coaching stock out of the original Fort William
terminus. Road transport prevailed over railway, and this site
is now the town's bypass. A new station was built in 1975
quite close to the former motive power depot, which itself is
now a large supermarket and bus station.
Photo: W.A.C. Smith © Transport Treasury

FORT WILLIAM

ACFI FEED=WATER HEATER

APPARATUS FITTED TO 4-4-2 AND 4-6-0 TYPES OF THE L.N.E.R.

ARTICLE REPRODUCED FROM THE RAILWAY ENGINEER, JULY 1928.

By the courtesy of Mr. H. N. Gresley, C.B.E., Chief Mechanical Engineer of the London & North Eastern Railway, we are enabled to reproduce a photograph of a 4-6-0 type express locomotive in service in the North Eastern Area, which, with another of the same class, has been fitted with the A.C.F.I. feed-water heating apparatus. Mr. Gresley, has, in addition, applied the same apparatus to engines of the 4-4-2 type belonging to the class originally built at Stratford for the Great Eastern Railway.

The apparatus comprises a heater consisting of two cylindrical tanks communicating with each other by means of a pipe. One of these tanks, 'A1', forms the heater proper, in which the feed water to be heated comes in direct contact with the exhaust steam which has been freed from grease by passing through an oil separator contained in this tank. The other tank, 'A2', divided into three compartments, forms the chamber for degasification and distribution of the feed water. A steam regulator is fitted on the pipe leading from the blast pipe to the heater and consists of a valve balanced by a spring which tends to keep it open. The regulator is controlled by a piston on which the pressure of the exhaust steam acts in the opposite direction to the spring.

A horizontal tandem pump is fitted, this consisting of a steam cylinder, driving direct two water cylinders in tandem, one for hot water and the other for cold, the latter having a much larger delivery than the former. The cold water from the tender is fed by gravity to a suction reservoir, as also is the hot water overflow from the feed heater. It is from this reservoir that the feed is taken for the cold cylinder of the pump. A steam cock is fitted to the live steam admission pipe of the pump to permit regulation of the pump speed to the demand. A mechanical lubricator, controlled by the hydraulic pressure of the pump, works

Holden Class B12 4-6-0 No. 8548 is shown with its A.C.F.I. equipment which was fitted to the loco in October 1931. Note that this is not the photograph referenced in the text above. © *Transport Treasury*

DIAGRAM SHOWING ARRANGEMENT OF A.C.F.I. FEED WATER HEATER

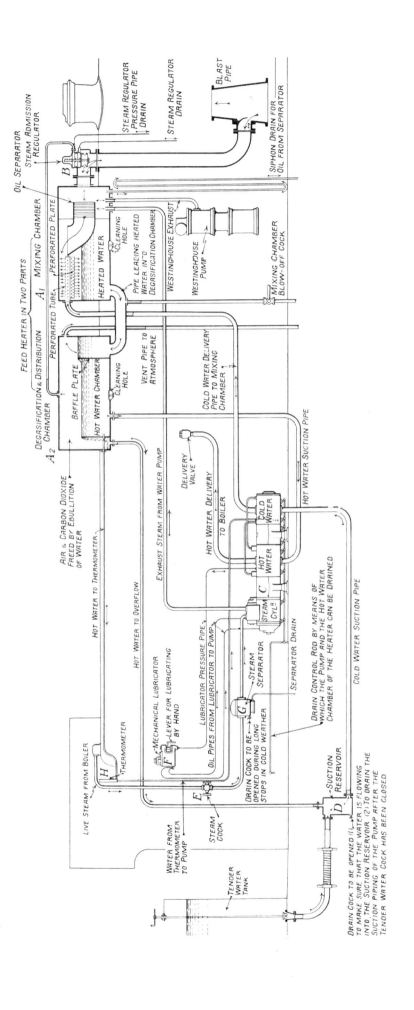

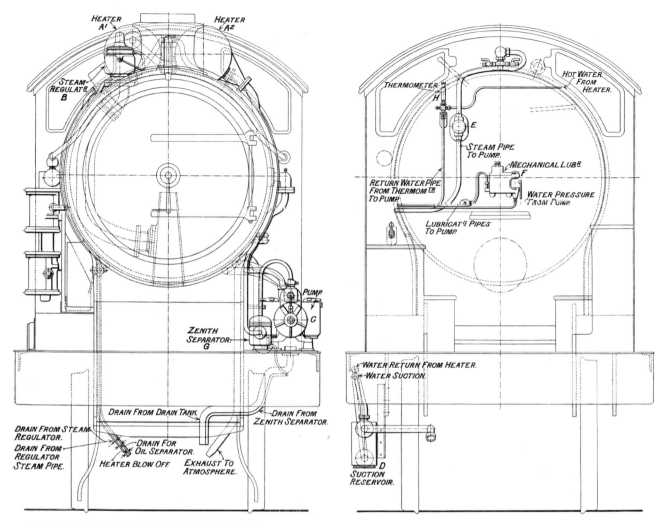

CROSS SECTIONAL DRAWINGS SHOWING GENERAL ARRANGEMENT OF A.C.F.I. FEED WATER HEATING APPARATUS

synchronously with the pump. A separator for the live steam pipe to pump is situated between the steam cock and the pump. A thermometer, fitted in the cab, indicates the water temperature.

Cold water from the tender flows by gravity to the suction reservoir 'D', where it is pumped up by the cold cylinder of the tandem pump 'C', and delivered into the mixing chamber of the feed heater 'A1', where it is forced in vertical jets through a perforated tube. The jets break up on the upper surface of the chamber and fall in fine rain through a perforated plate, thus raising the temperature rapidly to 212°F (100°C). The heated water is forced into the degasification chamber 'A2' by the slight pressure in the mixing chamber, and flows in a thin stream over the edge of a baffle plate into the hot water compartment. The dissolved gases liberated by the heat pass through a vent

pipe to the atmosphere. Since the delivery from the cold cylinder of the pump is greater than that of the hot cylinder, it follows that at each stroke of the pump an excess of water flows into the hot water compartment, the amount being further increased by the condensed exhaust steam. The water flows from the hot water compartment to the hot cylinder of the pump which feeds it to the boiler, while the excess water falls over into the third compartment of the degasification chamber and thence flows by gravity into the suction reservoir, from which it is again pumped by the cold water cylinder. This arrangement allows the hot water chamber to be kept continually filled and assures a full and constant feed.

The exhaust steam is admitted from the blast pipe into the mixing chamber 'A1' of the feed heater, through the steam regulator 'B'. This regulator maintains in the heater a constant low pressure sufficient to assure the combination of water and steam, and also keeps the amount of steam admitted proportional to the volume of water to be heated. At the same time, the arrangement for the flow of water from the mixing chamber to the degasification chamber 'A2' makes loss of steam impossible. The exhaust steam from the Westinghouse donkey pump and the tandem pump is led into the mixing chamber, through the oil separator, thus increasing the efficiency of the system. The heating of the feed water to the desired degree takes place automatically, the steam admitted to the heater varying with the quantity of water introduced. Consequently, when the pump is set to feed in proportion to the mean steam consumption of the locomotive a continuous feed is assured, and usually no attention is required between two consecutive stops.

Holden Class B12 4-6-0 No. 8569 seen departing Sheringham with a through train to Liverpool Street. Fitted with the apparatus in May 1932, the loco would only be in this guise until removal in December 1933. *Photo: A.W.V. Mace © Transport Treasury*

ELEVATION AND PLAN DRAWINGS SHOWING GENERAL ARRANGEMENT OF A.C.F.I. FEED WATER HEATING APPARATUS

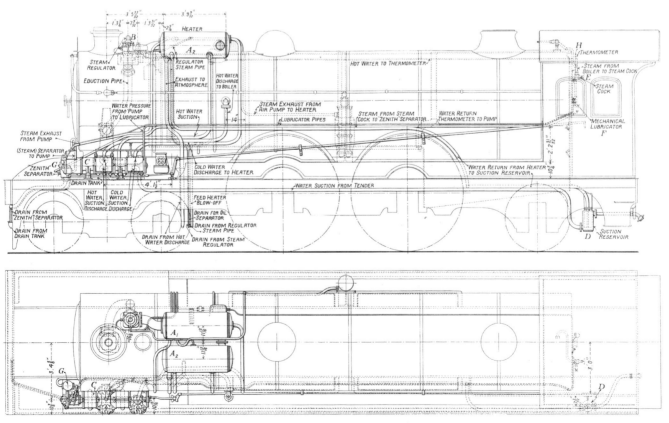

THE MASTER CUTLER

Thompson Class B1 4-6-0 No. 61376 of Leicester Central (38C) is pictured south of Rugby working hard on the Sheffield Victoria to Marylebone 'The Master Cutler'. Introduced by the LNER in 1947 and continued by the Eastern Region of British Railways, the service departed Sheffield Victoria at 7.40am calling at Nottingham Victoria, Leicester Central and Rugby Central, arriving at Marylebone at 11.15am, the return working departing at 6.15pm, arriving in Sheffield at 10.02pm. The downgrading of the GC main line saw the service transferred to Kings Cross in 1958 with the service running for a further ten years before being discontinued in 1968. *Photo: A.W.V. Mace © Transport Treasury*

THE QUEEN'S VISIT TO STRATFORD DEPOT IN 1962

BY DAVE BRENNAND

The Royal Family have been great ambassadors for UK railways for over 180 years, ever since Queen Victoria travelled by royal saloon on the Great Western Railway on the 13th June 1842. Her arrival at Paddington would have been the best publicity the GWR could have possibly dreamed of under the auspices of its greatest engineer Isambard Kingdom Brunel. Our railways and the Royal Family have always been intertwined. This short article looks back at a most memorable occasion on the 15th February 1962 when Her Majesty Queen Elizabeth II visited Stratford Depot including the High Meads Diesel Repair Shop, Temple Mills Marshalling Yard and the newly rebuilt Barking station.

The Royal party was conveyed in a special train which departed Liverpool Street at 2.25 pm, hauled by Brush Type 2 (Class 31) No. D5695. It is believed that the train, driven by Stratford driver Jack Searle, would have been propelled into Stratford Depot from Temple Mills East junction, stopping at a specially constructed platform for the Royal party to disembark within the depot. Shortly before this event, the Liverpool Street Division's most famous District Running & Maintenance Engineer, the late Richard Hardy, had been promoted to oversee the changeover from steam to diesel; a task which he carried out in a most admirable way. Steam had almost been eradicated by the time of the Queen's visit, but several examples were on display alongside the fleet of new diesels. According to R. H. N. Hardy's book 'Steam in the Blood', Her Majesty showed a genuine interest in the workings of the depot, its huge workforce and sprawling site. R. Hardy accompanied the Queen during part of her tour of Stratford and Dr. Richard Beeching was also present.

Many hundreds of the Depot's workforce turned out to welcome the Royal visitor as she toured the new B&C diesel shed, which was alongside the remains of the former Jubilee steam shed. Her Majesty was photographed many times during her visit, not just by official photographers, but also by the depot's employees. The party spent some time inside the cavernous High Meads Diesel Repair Shop

The Royal train departs from Liverpool Street on 15th February 1962 with Brush Type 2 D5695 at its head. It looks as though Stratford's legendary painters have been busy!
Photo: BR official

which had been converted to maintain an ever-growing fleet of diesels arriving from several manufacturers. The steam era fitters had spent the last few years learning how to maintain and repair an entirely new form of traction; a challenge which the majority certainly embraced. There was no choice; steam had served East Anglia well since the birth of railways, and the Great Eastern Division of BR was the first large area to see its complete eradication by September 1962. A plan which had its seeds sown by the Modernisation Plan for British Railways of 1955/56. The GE Division was at the forefront of the plan with widespread electrification and modernisation in the North-East London and Essex areas.

The young Queen had only been on the throne for ten years at the time of her visit. She looked resplendent and happy, gaining cheers wherever she roamed. There cannot be another Monarch in history who had such high regard worldwide and her passing on 8th September 2022 will be ingrained in our memories forever. Richard Hardy recalled that Her Majesty's visit was one of the highlights of his career and she was undoubtedly Stratford's most famous visitor.

The love and affection that railway enthusiasts and employees had for Stratford Depot was proven by an unveiling ceremony of a commemorative plaque in the new Stratford International station on the 10th July 2012, when over 200 former employees attended, including a speech by the legendary Richard Hardy who was by then in his early 90s.

The Queen's visit lasted almost an hour and promptly at 3.26 pm the train left Stratford Depot for the short trip to Temple Mills Yard. Another specially constructed wooden platform awaited the Royal visitor and her entourage of British Railways officials. Dr. Beeching, Chairman of the British Transport Commission and the ER General Manager Mr. J. R. Hammond (MBE) presented Her Majesty to the Yard Master and his team of engineers, control tower operators and inspectors. She was also shown, from the lofty Control Tower, the operation of the primary and secondary retarders (see page 31) which slowed down the loose wagons after they had been pushed over the hump and the directing of wagons into their assigned roads of which there were no less than 49 to choose from.

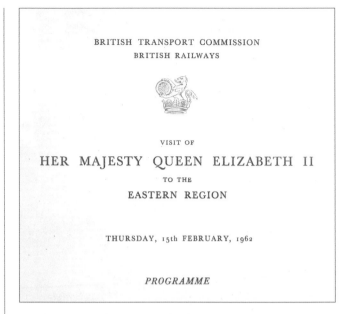

BRITISH TRANSPORT COMMISSION
BRITISH RAILWAYS

VISIT OF

HER MAJESTY QUEEN ELIZABETH II

TO THE

EASTERN REGION

THURSDAY, 15th FEBRUARY, 1962

PROGRAMME

Top: The booklet shown was handed out to members of staff on the day of the Queen's visit. Its contents have proven to be a most useful aid in the compilation of this article.

Bottom:
A very proud Royal Train driver, Jack Searle, meets the Queen.

Mr. P. Gray, the Works Manager, escorts Her Majesty around the Diesel Repair Shop.

This view was taken during the Queen's visit to the High Meads Diesel Repair Shop and she can be glimpsed amongst the crowd. Over 230 engineers and fitters worked here at this time and the much higher level of cleanliness required for diesel traction is evident.

The statistics surrounding the redevelopment of Temple Mills Marshalling yard are very impressive. The creation of goods sidings on the site dated back to the 1880s when the Great Eastern Railway's freight traffic was increasing year on year. The company gradually added extra yards to cope with increasing volumes of freight traffic. This created a haphazard system involving complex movements of wagons between the eight different yards to build up train formations for onward journeys. Decades later, this same complexity was still being perpetuated until the Modernisation Plan of the mid-1950s came to the rescue with a £3 million scheme to create one of the most modern hump shunting yards in the country. During the 4-year

period of reconstruction, some freight traffic had to be redirected to Bishopsgate, Thames Wharf, Goodmayes and other local yards. The new yard opened in September 1958 using the latest technology to speed up the flow of freight, which was a profitable business then. Sadly, during the 1970s and 80s, a massive decline in wagonload freight and the container revolution saw Temple Mills become a very overgrown and underused wasteland. Today, the whole site has undergone a multi-million pound redevelopment for a second time, to create the giant Eurostar servicing depot, which opened in 2007. Slightly to the north, new sidings were opened at Orient Way in 2008 for storage and cleaning of Abellio Greater Anglia

A view of the new Temple Mills Marshalling Yard looking towards Stratford, with the yard layout shown below.

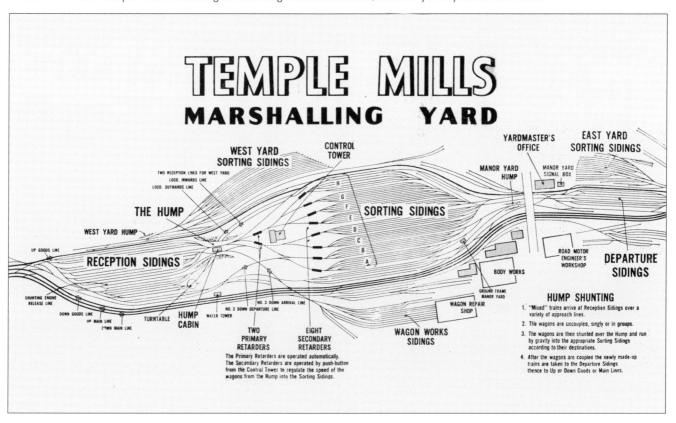

Clearly not the Royal Train, but pictures of it here at South Tottenham station are very elusive. The view here looking east, shows the branch towards Tottenham South Junction on the right. The line towards Woodgrange Park and Barking snakes off to the left. LMS Fowler designed 4F 0-6-0 No. 43924 heads towards Temple Mills in 1961. *Photo: Geoff Silcock*

electric units. Lea Bridge station, which had been closed since 1985, has undergone an expensive rebirth. After laying dormant for three decades, the station reopened in May 2016. The bygone sounds of loose coupled freight trains passing through Temple Mills have been replaced by a smoother, quieter and cleaner form of traction, but it is most doubtful that future generations will look back at these with the same fondness and nostalgia we feel for the steam and diesel era.

Returning to the Royal visit, once Her Majesty had spent some 40 minutes visiting Temple Mills and the Control Tower, at precisely 4.23pm the Royal train departed Temple Mills for the short trip to South Tottenham, where the engine ran round the train for the onwards journey to Barking via the former Tottenham and Forest Gate Joint line. During this section of the journey, as the train passed through the suburbs of Walthamstow and Leytonstone with fine views of the rooftops of thousands of terraced houses from the elevated line, afternoon tea was served on the train.

The 1950s reconstruction project in the Barking area of the London, Tilbury & Southend lines of the Eastern Region was required to alleviate the many delays caused by London Underground and BR passenger and freight services competing for routes across level junctions. The addition of two flyovers at the London end and a dive under for LU trains at the country end of the station solved these delays by segregating LU and BR services. Services were further enhanced by electrification and new electric multiple units, which were gradually introduced from November 1961.

Barking station's platforms and street level building were completely rebuilt, and the new station was officially opened on 29th September 1961 by the Mayor of Barking. The project was made even more remarkable by the fact that near normal train services ran throughout the many years of reconstruction and resignalling. The Royal train arrived at Barking at 5.05 pm after a brief pause on Barking Flyover so that officials could explain the background of the project to Her Majesty. The tour concluded with a visit to the new booking office and signal box. Over 20 employees were introduced to The Queen including the train crew. The Royal train driver was Jack Searle whom I had the pleasure of knowing in the early 1970s. He was a true gentleman, highly professional, well dressed and the perfect candidate for what was always considered, in footplate terms, to be the highest accolade. Jack was a prolific photographer of locomotives and sold his pictures to fellow footplate staff at Stratford. He even continued this practice after he retired. During our younger days, we must have both had blood transfusions with Type 'R' blood. 'R' of course, stands for RAILWAYS!

The newly constructed Barking Flyover is seen on the 29th March 1959, as Brush Type 2 A1A-A1A No. D5501 is seen propelling an engineer's train towards Barking station. The crew would have been in the other cab. *Photo: Author's Collection*

CONCRETE SIGNALS

Among the many shortages that occurred on the 'home front' during WW1 was that of timber. Timber was an essential component in many aspects of the railway, the most obvious being for sleepers and also in rolling stock constructions.

Dealing with sleepers first, many of these had been imported for some time and consequently there were now often delays in securing supplies. Sleepers were also required for the lines laid serving the front and in consequence some minor railways were literally picked up and moved for the duration. Perhaps the best known of these was the 'Basingstoke & Alton' line in rural Hampshire which would be immortalised (having been relaid) in later years as a result of 'Oh! Mr Porter'.

Another area in which there was a shortage related to signal posts. A 30 foot post required a fair size hardwood tree and again most of the railway companies were seeking similar. Enter upon the scene then one William Marriott, perhaps best described as an 'engineer extraordinaire'.

William Marriott was born in Basle, Switzerland in 1857. One could almost have anticipated the young William would be a gifted child for his father was a professor at the local university. Sadly as a boy he would also witness tragedy in his young life, for in 1868 aged just 11 he was orphaned. He left Switzerland soon after moving to Bideford, presumably with relatives although this is not stated. Tragedy seems not to have affected the young William for he was educated in both England and France and considered of sufficient ability to be taken on as a pupil at the engineering firm Ransomes & Rapier Ltd. in Ipswich between 1875 and 1879. Again it appears he was well regarded for after completing his training he commenced work as a draughtsman in 1880.

It appears William was contemplating making his fortune in America but in 1881 heard of a vacancy for an assistant engineer with Messrs Wilkinson & Jarvis, who were then constructing the Lynn & Fakenham, and Yarmouth & North Norfolk lines.

Perhaps there was some doubt as to his ability or maybe it was his young age, he was then just 24, but he was taken on trial by Jarvis – unpaid – for six weeks working mainly in the Yarmouth area, after which he was offered the permanent post.

During that trial time he assisted Mr. Jarvis with construction at the Yarmouth end and was then offered a permanent post which he took, giving up all idea of going to America. Thus, in 1883, he found himself Engineer, and a year later Locomotive Superintendent, of the Eastern & Midlands Railway. At the age of 26 he was possibly the youngest Engineer of a public railway since the days of Stephenson and Brunel. He carried his dual role throughout the M&GN period and in addition became Traffic Manager from January 1919 until his retirement at the end of 1924 by which time the company had been absorbed into the LNER. He died at Sheringham on 17th November 1943.

Marriott was one who recognised the potential in concrete for railway use. Concrete was already in use for bridges and even viaducts, for example Glenfinnan (Scotland) 1898, and before this Shawford (Hampshire) in 1891, although in the latter case the piers are faced with brick.

Marriott was of the opinion that concrete might well be used for lineside fittings, gateposts, signals, etc. and accordingly having established a concrete works at Melton Constable, registered patents for a number of uses and designs.

- **13,194** Improvements in or relating to reinforcements for reinforced concrete constructions. Applied 15th September 1915 – accepted 15th September 1916.

- **15,884** of 1915 for Reinforced concrete posts, etc.

- **104,224** Improvements in or relating to the metal reinforcements of reinforced concrete constructions. Applied 1st March 1916 – accepted 1st March 1917.

- **110,570** Improvements in or relating to reinforcements for reinforced concrete constructions Applied 20th October 1916 – accepted 22nd October 1917.

Concrete post and somersault starting signal in the 'off' position.
Notice too the concrete level crossing post behind, the latter painted.

- **135,599** Reinforced concrete posts, etc. 27th November 1918 Reinforced concrete beams

- **153,991** Improvements in or relating to the metal reinforcements of reinforced concrete constructions. Applied 1st September 1919. Published 25th November 1920.

- **165,884** Improvements in or relating to reinforced concrete posts, poles and the like. Applied 10th January 1920. Published 11th July 1921.

- **181,408** Improvements in or relating to moulding or forming concrete blocks and the like with Arthur William Roy and Albert Ramm. Applied 17th August 1921. Published 22nd June 1922.

- **516,722** Improvements in and relating to shuttering for casting concrete in situ. Applied 6th July 1938. Published 10th January 1940.

- Other, unrelated to concrete, patents are also registered to his name.

In consequence his many achievements include some of the first practical prefabricated concrete items. Away from civil engineering he was responsible for the design and construction of several locomotives, but perhaps his most difficult task was the efficient servicing of a railway run on a shoestring budget. The M&GN was indeed fortunate to have Marriott as its engineer as he was regarded with a kindly and indulgent eye from Derby, and what he asked for he usually got.

Heckington, east of Boston. Concrete signal post – this time without a cap – and unpainted level crossing post. Slight confusion with the 'Way Out' arrow and the 'No Exit' signs!

A lower height post. Aside from timber and concrete, the only alternative for a signal post was metal, invariably a lattice although it should be noted the SR did have rail built signals with two rails bolted together. Lattice posts were to be seen in use in a number of areas, and with different companies, perhaps the best known was the Stevens lattice used by the LSWR but it should be noted other manufacturers produced similar work each having slight design variations. The location of this photograph is unrecorded, do any readers know where it might be?

Marriott designs for concrete signal posts resulted in these being seen all over the M&GN system, indeed concrete signal posts would similarly become a feature on many LNER lines later. Other companies, notably the Great Western attempted to copy his ideas, presumably taking care not to infringe the patent, but they were not so fortunate and although the concrete was successfully cast on the ground it was the vibration created moving to site and subsequent erection that created problems, cracks created which led to ingress of water and consequent cracking and scoring. (The Cambrian lines post grouping had perhaps the most concrete signals on any part of the GWR, the explanation being that when the Cambrian company realised they would not exist after 1923 they simply reduced signal post replacement to the minimum leaving the new owners [Paddington] with a backlog of work).

- The word 'Midland' in the title of the M&GN railway and the relationship that existed between the two led to Derby casting concrete signal posts for use by the Great Northern and similarly at Gorton for the Great Central as timber shortages built up towards the end of WW1. Although not stated, it is reasonable to assume these were to the Marriott patent and consequently suitable royalties were paid. It also goes to explain the presence of concrete post signals on the respective systems.

A somersault distant signal, the post having several guy wires attached.

- Most concrete post GWR signals had disappeared by the 1960s although examples of the concrete type on the LNER (the M&GN system having closed in 1959). were still present into the 1990s.

- One advantage of the concrete post, and which in this respect was similar to timber, was that the necessary fittings might be added at any number of points, either by clamp or through holes specifically included in the post. The latter also acted to reduce wind pressure. Actual fittings might also result in upper, lower or somersault signals; all suitable for a Marriott concrete post.

- Returning to the man himself, Marriott was at first regarded kindly as the 'young Guv'nor'. He was perhaps best described as Victorian; courteous and humane with a practical and unselfconscious sense, different indeed to many; his contemporary Dugald Drummond perhaps his polar opposite. As he aged he became perhaps more stern but was still seen as the figurehead of the M&GN as indeed he was.

- Sadly Marriott's true legacy, the M&GN system was closed by British Railways in 1959 but his name at least lives on in Marriott Way, Sheringham.

References: Steam index.

'A Biographical Dictionary of Railway Engineers'. John Marshall. David & Charles 1978.

'A Pictorial Record of LNER Constituent Signalling'. A. A. Maclean. OPC 1983.

(Marriott's concrete signal posts are described in detail by Nigel J. L. Digby in 'Railway Archive', (11), 77.)

(All images, the late Gresham Smith courtesy Richard Sissons. No dates/locations recorded.)

An upper quadrant arm and white painted post –
the pole route and wires a memory of times past.

J37 AT STANNERGATE

William Reid designed Class J37 0-6-0 No. 64620 pictured at Stannergate, Dundee heading towards Broughty Ferry with the daily goods service to Montrose on 10th January 1967.

Around this time only a handful of J37 0-6-0s remained active and this was one of their last regular workings, leaving Dundee each morning around 11.30am. Their other workings were the local goods to Maryfield in Dundee and the Tayport pick-up goods, both of which ran only as required and were often alternatively powered by a Dundee B1. Diesels took over the Montrose goods in April 1967.

No. 64620 had been built for the North British Railway by the North British Locomotive Company at their Atlas Works and introduced to service as No. 110 in December 1920. 46 years and 4 months later the loco was withdrawn on 22nd April 1967, being one of the final steam locomotives in service on BR Scottish Region. In September 1967 No. 64620 was cut up at Motherwell Machinery and Scrap (Wishaw).

The line pictured was part of the Dundee & Arbroath Railway which opened in 1838, it used the unusual track gauge of 5ft 6in but was converted to standard gauge in 1848 enabling it to connect with the emerging Scottish railway network. It was absorbed by the larger Caledonian Railway, but when the North British Railway completed the construction of the Tay Bridge in 1878, it was granted part ownership of the line to enable it to form its main line to Aberdeen, so the line became the Dundee and Arbroath Joint Line, an arrangement which continued until the 1923 Grouping.

ASPECTS OF THE MABLETHORPE LOOP

BY NICK DEACON

SOME EARLY L&ECR HISTORY.

Driven by the vigour of Victorian entrepreneurial optimism the Louth to Mablethorpe line had started life as the Louth & East Coast Railway (L&ECR) authorised in July 1872 although matters lapsed until May 1877 when a second Act was passed to extend the time needed for land purchase and construction. Prompted by local businessmen and farmers, nevertheless the increasing holiday traffic enjoyed by Mablethorpe and its neighbour Sutton-le-Marsh (soon to be more attractively named Sutton-on-Sea) must have also provided motivation for the new railway. Prior to the arrival of the railway day trippers and holiday makers had to use an inconvenient omnibus service from Alford station on the East Lincolnshire Railway (ELR).

When completed by contractor Henry Jackson and opened on 16th October 1877 the single track line ran for 11 miles 68 chains departing from the ELR at Mablethorpe Junction, a little over a mile south of Louth station. (The ELR had opened in 1848, but was worked from the start by the Great Northern Railway (GNR) and remained independent until the 1923 Grouping when it became a part of the LNER.) Crossing unchallenging country of pasture land, criss-crossed by drainage dykes, where the steepest gradient was 1 in 132, en route there were twelve level crossings (these were mostly manned and with crossing keeper's houses) and six under bridges, the latter of all-wood construction. Substantial single-platformed brick-built two-storey station buildings incorporating the station master's accommodation plus modest sidings, cattle pens, loading docks, weigh houses and signal boxes were provided at Grimoldby, Saltfleetby and Theddlethorpe. At Louth a bay was added to the south end of the Up platform for the branch services and in 1887 a new 51-lever signal box (later reduced to 43 levers) named Louth South was also added to the same platform. The existing 53-lever

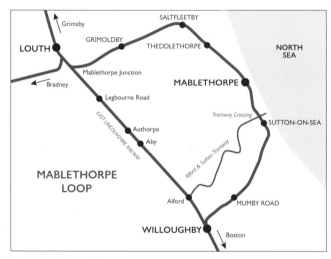

A c.1908 view of the superb ELR station at Louth featuring the neo-Jacobean architectural embellishments and the large porte cochère (covered carriage) entrance. Also of note are the curved red brick stone-capped gables and the balustrade roof with linked chimney stacks. After closure as a passenger station in 1970 and granted a Grade II listing in 1974, the building was left derelict for many years and threatened with demolition. Fortunately good sense prevailed and it was saved, renovated, and converted into very tasteful residential accommodation.
Photo: Courtesy John Alsop

1656. Louth Station, Exterior.

At Louth on 16th May 1954, a nicely cleaned J6 0-6-0 No. 64199 of Colwick shed (38A) is in charge of the RCTS East Midlands Branch Nottinghamshire – Lincolnshire rail tour which commenced at Nottingham Midland station with ex-LMS Compound 4-4-0 No. 40935 as far as Lincoln. According to the tour schedule the train (now with No. 64199 which had come on at Lincoln) had arrived 'wrong line' from the Bardney branch and next took the tour over the Mablethorpe Loop before heading back to Nottingham via Woodhall Junction, Bardney and Lincoln. The J6 lasted at Colwick, the largest shed on the former GNR system, until withdrawn in April 1958. The attractive overall roof, now looking dishevelled, was removed during the 1960s and replaced by two separate platform canopies.
Photo: Neville Stead © Transport Treasury

signalbox at the north end of the station was renamed Louth North on the same date.

To anticipate the expected throng of rail-borne summer holidaymakers and an on-going healthy build-up of goods traffic, the GNR strongly recommended that the terminus at Mablethorpe, being the railhead for the area be well equipped with four platforms, a generous goods depot equipped with a good range of sidings, a cattle dock, signal box, and a brick-built single road loco shed, with a slated gable roof measuring 60ft x 20ft complemented with a 44ft 8in locomotive turntable. The latter was extended by 1947 to 45ft 9in and again in 1954 by a 52ft model recovered from Doncaster. From the outset the line was worked by the GNR who undertook to provide the necessary motive power, rolling stock, staff, and an initial service of four passenger trains each way – all for 50% of the receipted income over twenty-one years.

ENTER THE S&WR AND THE GNR

The next enterprise to enter the stage meaningfully was the Sutton & Willoughby Railway (S&WR) which in conjunction with the 1884 North Sea Fisheries, Harbour & Dock Act sought to connect a proposed dock at Sutton-on-Sea with a 7 mile 13 chain line to the GNR at Willoughby. Complicating matters was the opening in April the same year of the 8 mile 2ft 6in gauge Alford & Sutton Tramway which ran from the ELR station yard at Alford through Bilsby, Markby and Hannah to terminate at the Jolly Bacchus Inn at Sutton. The tramway was a well-run and successful company but, despite offering opposition to the S&WR proposal, was doomed to failure when the latter received parliamentary blessing in July 1884. Work on the north-facing junction on the ELR at Willoughby started in June 1885 and a new 20-lever signal box was also added there in addition to the existing signal box at the station.

As shadows lengthen in the summer of 1938, C12 4-4-2T No. 4525 provides the centrepiece for this charming portrait as it waits to leave the Up platform bay at Louth with a train for Sutton-on-Sea. The loco was completed at Doncaster during August 1901 and was of an extremely useful class of sixty designed by H. A. Ivatt and built between 1898 and 1907. Becoming LNER No. 7379 in 1946 and BR No. 67379, she was a long term Louth shed (40C) resident until November 1955 when a brief move to Spital Bridge shed (35C) preceded her last move to New England shed (35A) where withdrawal occurred in June 1958. Beyond the train the single gable of the rear of the engine shed can be seen. *Photo: © RailOnline*

With no challenges provided by the topology of the route, the contractor James Dickson pressed ahead rapidly with construction of the line through to its formal opening on 23rd September 1886.

Although the formation was constructed to allow for double track, only single was ever laid. At Sutton-on-Sea there was a two-platform station with a passing loop and Mumby Road was the only other intermediate station but with a single platform and passing loop. Each was provided with sidings (four at Sutton and two at Mumby Road), a 1 ton 10 cwt crane, a timber goods shed and a weigh house each. Mumby Road was also provided with cattle pens but not at Sutton which did not handle livestock traffic. Along the route there were six level crossings, two over bridges and several under bridges carrying the line over the area's drains and dykes including one having an

81½ft span. At Willoughby a new and resited station with three platform faces replaced the original 1848 structure; the work being carried out by the GNR with the S&WR paying £3,966 towards the costs. Unlike the brick-built stations on the L&CER, the stations at Sutton and Mumby Road were of a single-storey wooden construction as was the ELR station at Willoughby. At Sutton and Mumby Road separate two-storey brick station master's houses built in the 1880's 'Arts and Craft' style were also provided. A bay on the north side of Willoughby station was added for terminating branch services.

For a while the Sutton & Alford tramway continued with the unequal struggle for traffic against competition from the S&WR and indifference by the GNR but finally closed its doors in December 1889 after the gap between Mablethorpe and Sutton-on-Sea was bridged by the

During the 1930s, the first of the ex-GCR Parker Class N5 0-6-2Ts came to Louth shed with a few more arriving in the early 1950s to replace elderly GNR types on goods, pilot, and passenger work. No. 69309, seen at the south end of the shed yard on 19th September 1954, had arrived from Immingham shed (40B) in July 1953 and stayed until November 1955 when it moved back to GCR territory at Staveley shed (38D), where it lasted until November 1960. Ex-GNR carriage stock for the Loop branch is seen at the bay behind the loco and looming over the scene is the monolithic concrete building of the ABM maltings which had replaced an earlier maltings that was destroyed in an air raid in 1940. Construction of the replacement began in 1949 with production commencing in 1952 and lasting until 1998. The building was demolished during 2014/15. *Photo: Neville Stead © Transport Treasury*

A portrait of ex-GCR Robinson J11 0-6-0 No. 64320 which was the last of the class to remain at Louth on closure of the shed in December 1956. It had arrived from Immingham in May 1948 and is seen at the north end of the shed on 19th September 1954 (probably on the occasion of a society visit) in the company of C12 4-4-2T No. 67383 which had barely four months left before withdrawal in January 1955. *Photo: Neville Stead © Transport Treasury*

It is hard to resist views of the much-loved C12 locos and another of the class, No. 67364, is seen at Louth on an unrecorded date during the 1950s, with sister loco No. 67384 lurking behind. Both engines were on 40C's strength in 1950 and both were withdrawn during May 1956 thus helping to narrow the date down somewhat. Forming the backdrop is the WW2 repaired brick wall of the station and the replacement shed entrance. *Photo: Neville Stead © Transport Treasury*

In the shed yard on an unknown date in the 1950s the GCR look is made up of N15 0-6-2T No. 69297 in company with an unidentified A5 4-6-2T, whilst J11 0-6-0 No. 64312 is stabled on the other side of the 49ft 8in turntable which was installed in 1938. The J11 type had first arrived in the early 1930s and the few that found a home at Louth through the years proved to be very popular with crews. *Photo: from an unknown source*

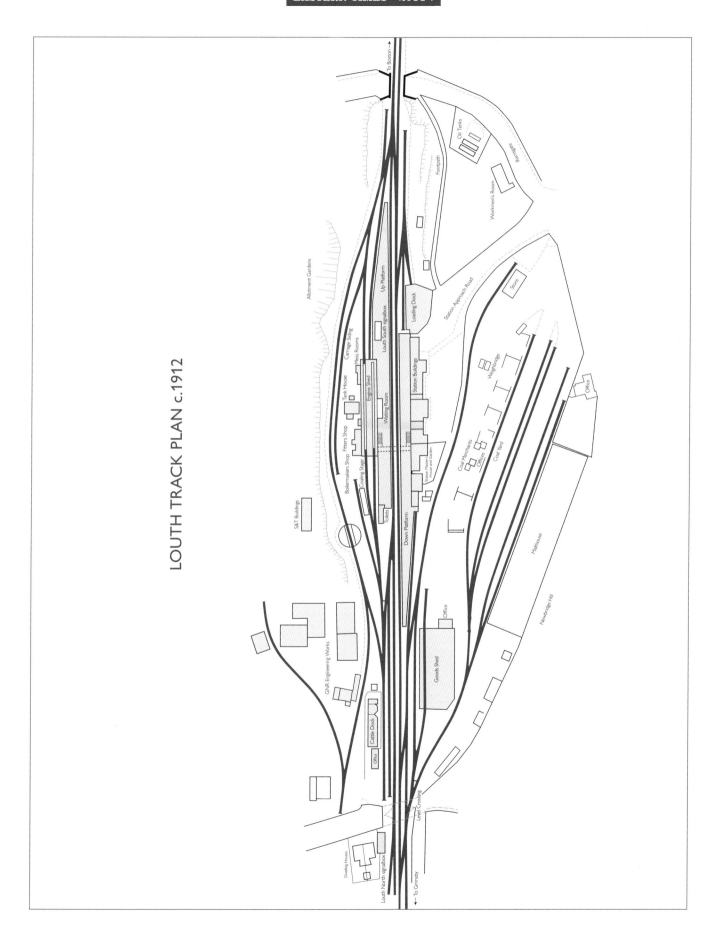

LOUTH TRACK PLAN c.1912

During 1956, the last year of C12 operations over the Loop, Louth's No. 67398 was the last of the class to remain at the shed before closure in December 1956 when the loco was moved to Immingham. Pictured here coming off the Loop at Mablethorpe Junction and heading along the Down main towards Louth, the fireman appears to have surrendered the single line token upon the reception post. The exquisite 18-lever Mablethorpe Junction box in this position dated from around 1906 when it was moved from the west to the east side of the line. The first 'box dating from 1877 was recorded as having 24 levers.

Photo from the Bill Woolhouse Collection © Lincolnshire Coast Light Railway (LCLR)

S&WR extension opened on 14th July 1888. This had crossed the tramway on the level to the north of Sutton-on-Sea station at a location known as Tramway Crossing which had been provided with a 7-lever signal box. The extension of the S&WR met the L&ECR with an end-on junction at Mablethorpe thus allowing through running to and from Louth and Willoughby, and for the privilege of using the station the S&WR paid the L&ECR an annual rent of £165. As with the L&ECR, the S&WR working arrangements for their line were dependent on the co-operation of the GNR and this was settled under the same terms as those agreed with the L&ECR. The initial timetable advertised five weekday only trains each way with these complemented by an immediate influx of holiday special excursions which set the scene for decades to come. In 1889 the GNR improved the accommodation facilities at Mablethorpe and at the same date probably added the footbridge at the south end of the station.

Although the completion of the loop proved to be a success and brought large numbers of seasonal visitors to Mablethorpe and Sutton-on-Sea, there was no progress on the proposed new dock at Sutton to which the GNR had shown, at best, only lukewarm support. The final nail in the port's coffin proved to be the financial collapse in 1897 of the Lancashire, Derby & East Coast Railway (LD&ECR) scheme which was supported by Derbyshire coal owners seeking to move their products through to the new dock at Sutton for export. This line reached out from Warrington on the Manchester Ship Canal through Derbyshire and Lincolnshire and sought to reach Sutton with a junction on the S&WR at Mumby Road. The scheme also included the LD&ECR takeover of both the L&ECR and S&WR. The line managed to reach Lincoln but there the money ran out and with the S&WR unable to repay its debt to the GNR, the Lincoln to Sutton-on-Sea section of the grandiose scheme was scrapped along with the port. After this failure, from 1900, the S&WR entered negotiations with the GNR with the aim of settling the outstanding financial issues and engineering a takeover deal. This was settled in March 1902 followed in 1904 with the possibility of a similar deal being broached by the L&EC. After some delay the necessary absorption bill was passed in August 1908 thus bringing both arms of the 'Loop' under the GNR umbrella.

SIGNALLING

The line was signalled with the distinctive GNR somersault post and arm type and each station was provided with a timber signal box with either a Stevens & Son lever frame for those on the L&ECR section or a Saxby & Farmer lever frame for those on the S&WR section. Given the GNR's penchant for contracting out the construction to local builders, although there was conformity to a general company style (e.g. 'Type 1b' specified for the Louth-Mablethorpe section), each structure had inbuilt detail differences depending on the whim of the builder. Working out in order from the 24-lever Mablethorpe Junction signal box to the south of Louth, Grimoldby had a 19-lever frame and was a block post only, Saltfleetby a 16-lever and Theddlethorpe a 19-lever frame. At Mablethorpe the first signalbox of 40-levers was probably moved to a new position in 1888 in conjunction with the S&WR extension from Sutton but retained the same Stevens lever size. Moving onto the S&WR, next was the Tramway Crossing signalbox dating from July 1888 with a 7-lever Saxby & Farmer frame, followed by Sutton-on-Sea with a 16-lever, then Mumby Road with a 14-lever and finally the 20-lever frame Willoughby Junction signalbox on the ELR. Train operations on the single line sections were controlled by staff and ticket regulations on the Louth to Mablethorpe section and by electric tablet on the Mablethorpe to Willoughby section with the change-over for through trains passing from one section to another managed by Mablethorpe signal box.

MOTIVE POWER

Early loco power provided by the GNR would have been based at Louth shed – a two-road brick-built structure measuring 170ft x 30ft having a slated, single pitch gable roof with arched entrances. Opened by the ELR in 1848, the first allocation would have consisted of Sharp, Hawthorn and Sturrock 0-4-2, 2-4-0, 0-6-0 and 0-4-2T types with these increasingly replaced by Patrick Stirling's first Doncaster products. One loco was also outstationed at the sub-shed at Mablethorpe which had opened in 1877. For many years the loco was Stirling 0-4-2 No. 958 followed in the 1920s by C12 4-4-2T No. 4506. In February 1906 GNR steam railmotor No. 8 built by Avonside Engine Co. joined forces with two others at Louth specifically for work on the Loop services. However, due to their inability to haul more than one carriage when demand exceeded their seating capacity of around 50, they were withdrawn from the service from September 1914 and replaced with conventional locos and carriages. Just prior to 1923 the Louth allocation stood at seven: three C12 4-4-2Ts, one each of the D2 and D3 4-4-0s and two E1 2-4-0s, but in 1931 had grown to around sixteen with eight classes represented including six C12, three D2, two D3 and single examples of classes J10/11/52/65 and 69. By this date operations on the Loop were characterised by the popular C12 4-4-2Ts which had first arrived in 1920 and staying in diminishing numbers until the closure of Louth shed (now coded 40C) in December 1956. In 1950 the allocation stood at a solitary D3 4-4-0 (No. 62132) two J11 0-6-0s, one N15 and no less than seven C12s. The last C12 on the books was No. 67398 which on closure of the shed in December 1956 was transferred first to Immingham shed (40B) and finally to New England (35A) where it lasted until November 1958. In BR days the C12s were eagerly sought out by rail enthusiasts wherever they were based and particularly at Louth. Here, apparently, it was the custom for those in the know to leave Up stopping services at the station, dash madly to the platform end where the official access to the shed was, then through the shed to view any

of the class and then return at top speed to regain the train – hopefully before it had departed! As the C12s disappeared they were replaced by ex-GCR N5 0-6-2Ts with seven of the class arriving at different dates during the late 1940s/1950s. No. 69322 was the last to remain just prior to the shed's closure. From time to time during the 1950s ex-GCR A5 4-6-2Ts arrived on short term loans from Boston, Immingham, and Lincoln sheds with Nos. 69803/4/12/16 amongst those known to have been used on the Loop services.

Mablethorpe shed had closed as far back as June 1924 but because steam locos continued to arrive until 1967 it continued as a servicing depot. In fact, such was the increase of holiday traffic during the 1950s which now employed longer wheelbase locos, in 1954 BR needed to replace the 45ft 9in turntable with one of 52ft recovered from Doncaster in order to avoid a 15 mile trip to turn on the Firsby triangle. However, although the LMS Black 5 4-6-0s with a 51ft 2¾in wheelbase could just about squeeze on, the practice for these locos was to continue using the Firsby triangle. Perhaps it was a question of difficulty in balancing the locos on the turntable or even reluctance on the part of the Eastern Region to allow this particular class use of this particular turntable!

Lincoln-based Craven, Derby and Metro-Cammell DMU sets commenced working the Loop from 1956 and one of the Derby 'whiskered' sets is seen at the single-platformed Grimoldby station with a service to Grimsby Town via Louth. The service was probably one of the late afternoon/early evening departures from Willoughby and one wonders at this time whether any passengers alighted or joined the service! The fine station building, floral platform displays and GNR lamp standard are particularly noteworthy. The station was the boyhood home of actor Donald Pleasence whose father was stationmaster there during the inter-war years. *Photo: © Transport Treasury*

THE GROUPING, LNER AND BR YEARS.

Over the years the basic Louth to Willoughby passenger timetable tended to vary, based around a core service of between seven to ten trains per day, but with some of these running between Sutton or Mablethorpe to Louth only and Mablethorpe to Willoughby only. During the summer seasons holiday traffic to Mablethorpe continued to grow exponentially with excursion and holiday specials arriving regularly from Leicester Belgrave Road, Nottingham Victoria, Derby Friargate, further afield and of course from Kings Cross, London. As an example, 92,000 holiday makers were recorded as visiting Mablethorpe in 1906. During the Great War traffic was heavy with the line having become the focus for troops moving to training camps in the area. In 1922 Bradshaw's reflected a slight reduction in the Louth weekday departures to a total of six with only two of these, the 7.42am and the 5.35pm, being through services to Willoughby while the other services terminated at either Mablethorpe or Sutton-on-Sea and

one of these, the 2.10pm to Mablethorpe, was a Thursday only service. By comparison, the same timetable showed Willoughby with nine departures with only two of these, the 1.10pm and the 7.20pm, running through to Louth. Two of the other departures were Saturday only through trains from Nottingham and one other was a Friday only service, also from Nottingham. Other timetable nuances included morning services commencing from Mablethorpe and Sutton to Louth and Willoughby. The GNR was not slow in marketing the charms of Mablethorpe advertising it amongst other colourful poster blandishments as 'Safe, Sunny, Salubrious – Merry Mablethorpe – the Children's Playground'. Other richly illustrated advertising material extolled Mablethorpe's claims to be an 'unrivalled health resort', enjoying 'the lowest rainfall on the East Coast' and the 'maximum hours of sunshine'. Similar colour poster themes of a slightly less exuberant nature were employed by the LNER and with even more restraint by BR. During the inter-war

A delightful pre-1914 view of the tranquil bucolic charm of Theddlethorpe station. Watched by the station master, the signalman and possibly the one potential passenger, a Louth-bound service arrives hauled by what appears to be a Stirling tender engine.
Photo: Courtesy John Alsop

A late afternoon panoramic view of Mablethorpe station looking north from the footbridge where Richard Morton and his cousin spent such an enjoyable afternoon in 1964. Out of sight to the left and behind the goods shed is the site of the engine shed. A Cravens 2-car DMU awaits departure from platform 2 – a type which had entered service between 1956 and 1959 and used extensively throughout eastern England. Also on the same platform is the famous W.H. Smith bookstall which also sold toys and books, arranged newspaper deliveries around the town and was regarded very much as a local community amenity. *Photo: Ken Courscy © Transport Treasury*

years holiday traffic continued to grow with numbers arriving at Mablethorpe reaching a peak of 166,000 in 1936 and were hardly less during the 1950s with 136,400 recorded for 1959. From 1934 Theddlethorpe became a location within the LNER Camping Coach scheme and one coach was based in the siding during the summer season until 1939. During WW2 Louth, Mablethorpe and Sutton-on-Sea were targets of Luftwaffe hit and run raids; the most serious of these from a railway perspective was one carried out over Louth on 19th February 1941 which concentrated on the station and shed area. During the raid, which severely damaged the north end of the shed and the coal stage, fireman George Bradley, a local man who was on the footplate of a shunting loco in the goods yard, was unfortunately killed. The damaged arched entrances of the shed were replaced by a steel lintel supported by a brick column set between the two tracks but the coal stage was never restored and coaling was afterwards carried out direct from wagons. The damaged roof of the shed was also replaced with asbestos sheeting let in with glazed panels. During February 1953 the Loop became a lifeline when during the night of 31st January and 1st February severe flooding caused by high winds and a huge tidal surge breached many coastal defences between Lincolnshire and Kent with many towns inundated. In Lincolnshire, Mablethorpe and Sutton-on-Sea were particularly affected with flood waters reaching some two miles inland and reaching a depth of five to six feet in Mablethorpe and Sutton, resulting in wholesale evacuations to Alford and Louth. Forty-two people from the area also became victims. The permanent way between Mablethorpe and Sutton was also crippled with ballast and earthworks washed away. The emergency work, over the following two weeks or more, in-filling the breaches and repairing the sea wall defences in the area involved the Army and private contractors bringing in train loads of Scunthorpe slag plus chalk and stone from the Midlands.

DECLINE AND CLOSURE

Running through a sparsely populated area with declining traffic returns bolstered only by the influx of summer excursion revenue, a pragmatists view of the future of the Loop beyond the 1960s would have been less than optimistic. Despite the introduction of diesel stock on local passenger services, what was really needed was an injection of fresh management thinking to stimulate viability on at least the busier section of the route as a counter to the increase of private car ownership. This was particularly so with the Louth to Mablethorpe section which historically carried less holiday traffic and by the late 1950s was alleged to be losing around £9,500 per annum, and now required expensive repairs to certain sections of the permanent way. Even during the LNER period it was clear that traffic returns on the section were on the decline and other than a modest number of purely local passengers and the daily Louth-Willoughby pick-up goods service, little use was being made of the intermediate stations. With the seasonal holiday traffic increasingly

being routed via Willoughby, the nature of this part of the route as merely a tranquil rural crumb-catcher was emphasised even more. The increase of private car ownership during the 1950s pulled more passenger use away – so much so that some purely local trains were running virtually empty. The introduction of new Derby lightweight DMUs on all the east Lincolnshire area passenger services from 1956, although replacing the aging steam stock and enabling the closure of Louth engine shed, made little difference to traffic levels and in 1960 BR proposed the closure of the Louth to Mablethorpe section. Although inevitably there were hardship issues for the few who used the intermediate stations these were not enough to sway the East Midlands TUCC against the proposal. With not much than a murmur, closure quietly took place from Monday 5th December 1960 with the last train, a two-car DMU, running through to Willoughby

A fine study of LMS 'Crab' 2-6-0 No. 42847 at Mablethorpe station on Sunday 2nd August 1959 heading a southbound summer special. A trio of onlookers take advantage of the scene below them while the train is held at the crossing gates. At this date the loco was based at Nottingham Annesley shed (16D) and would have been rostered to bring in similar summer services from the Midlands until transferred briefly to Burton shed (17B) in June the following year and finally Gorton shed, Manchester (9G) where withdrawal occurred during June 1962. *Photo: Neville Stead © Transport Treasury*

the previous Saturday. The last Mablethorpe to Louth passenger service, which departed after the arrival of the last DMU from Louth, was a Peterborough–Grimsby service running via the Loop hauled by a B1 4-6-0.

A sweetener appeared to be offered by BR in the future retention of the Mablethorpe – Willoughby section with a promise of 'developing holiday traffic' to both Mablethorpe and Sutton-on-Sea in conjunction with similar attention given to other resorts such as Cleethorpes and Skegness. In the event this intention (if ever there was one) proved to be a falsehood with the shock announcement of the 1963 Beeching 'reshaping' plan which proposed the removal of most of East Lincolnshire from the passenger railway map. During the interim years between the closure of the Louth–Mablethorpe section and the publication of the plan, it was clear that BR had not made any effort to

'develop' holiday traffic – rather the opposite in fact with the reduction in the availability of cheaply priced excursion tickets, the withdrawal of services from the summer timetables, the cancellation of holiday advertising and guidebook literature and, for those services which remained, the substitution of standard carriage stock for those without corridor connections. No surprise then that BR could claim that fewer passengers were using the services and as a consequence 'hardship' suffered by the closures would be correspondingly less. Goods services were ceased with effect from 30th March 1964. Opposition to the proposals headed by the East Midlands TUCC, local MPs and local councils was bitter and prolonged, but despite two public enquiries held at Skegness in September 1964 and May 1968, 're-examinations' of the proposals by the Ministry of Transport and the BR Board, the closures were upheld with the exception of the Firsby to Skegness

Another Nottingham-based loco – this time Class B1 4-6-0 No. 61163 of Colwick shed (40E) – waits to leave Mablethorpe on Saturday 9th September 1961 with the 1.52pm departure for Leicester (Belgrave Road). The loco was new to traffic in May 1947 and started life at Gorton shed and remained on the GC section with moves to Neasden and Leicester until moved to Colwick during December 1954 where it remained until withdrawn during September 1962. Just visible is further evidence of a typically busy Saturday at Mablethorpe with at least two other locos waiting to return home with their summer specials. *Photo: Horace Gamble © Transport Treasury*

line which was to be retained. Closure was enacted as from Monday 5th October 1970 with the last trains running the previous Saturday. Given that during this period (despite the obstacles placed by BR) Mablethorpe was still managing to attract an embarrassingly high (to the BR Board at least!) level of rail-borne holiday traffic it was difficult to resist the logic that some level of retention underpinned by sensible economies was a sensible alternative. As it was, the closure decision was seen by many as at best, a shameful lack of judgement or, at worst, part of a cynical plan devised by powerful and politically supported lobby groups to drive more traffic onto the British road system.

After closure and demolition large parts of the route returned to farmland but tangible remains survive in the shape of the distinctive station buildings at Grimoldby, Saltfleetby and Theddlethorpe – all of which are now well cared for as domestic residences. Other surviving structures are the equally distinctive crossing keeper houses which continue as domestic residences. Those at Back Street, Eastfield Lane, Golf Road, Kent Avenue, Marr Dyke, and Tinkle Street are notable survivors. Mablethorpe station was regrettably demolished many years ago as were those at Sutton-on-Sea and Mumby Road.

A 1964 MABLETHORPE MEMORY

Railway enthusiast Richard Morton visited the resort with his parents, together with his cousin Peter, in the summer of 1964 and recalls one day spent watching trains at the station in preference to the pleasures to be had at the beach.

"It was a summer Saturday in 1964 on a typical east Lincolnshire summer's day, with the wind blowing strongly and clouds scudding across a blue, grey sky. There was even some sunshine although nobody would

On 24th April **1965** the Locomotive Club of Great Britain (LCGB) Nottinghamshire and Lincolnshire Railtour visited Mablethorpe as part of an extensive itinerary starting from London St Pancras and employing Britannia Pacific No. 70052 *Firth of Tay*, LMS 4F 0-6-0 No. 44401, B1 4-6-0 No. 61406 and Ivatt 4MT 2-6-0 No. 43108 from Canklow shed (41D), Rotherham. The Ivatt had taken over from the B1 at Skegness for the Mablethorpe leg of the tour and is seen after its mid-afternoon arrival at Mablethorpe prior to reversing with the train to Boston where the handover to the B1 occurred. *Photo: Alec Swain © Transport Treasury*

claim that it was warm. We'd walked up from the beach where our families were sheltering behind the obligatory wind breaks, but we'd decided to see what was happening at the station. We should have had platform tickets, but I don't think that we bought any and none of the staff challenged us - they smiled and got on with what would be a busy day. After wandering up and down the platforms, four in total, and looking at the signalbox with its odd plank bridge access over one of the unused bay platforms (No. 1) we climbed up onto the footbridge and stayed there until mid-afternoon when hunger demanded that we return to the beach and food.

Mablethorpe, in the state that we saw it then was a station in reverse – it was planned as a terminus from the line to Louth and, once that had closed, the north facing bays, Nos. 1 and 4, became useless for all practical purposes except storage. I've often wondered why platform 4 wasn't extended over the level crossing to meet the line from Sutton which would have given three through platforms. The station was on the outskirts of the town in those days, but Mablethorpe has since grown and the station's site is now virtually untraceable, apart from one remaining platform edge if you know where to look!

In a sense Mablethorpe's trains were a bit like the tides which came in and then went out again. First of all came half a dozen holiday extra trains from about 10 o'clock until lunchtime. None came from very far away, mostly being from the east Midlands such as Nottingham or Derby – we had no idea where Radford was. Leicester seemed the most remote with Sheffield not far behind; these last mentioned were last in. Motive power was mainly LM Region in origin which was surprising to us as we'd expected Eastern Region engines. Ivatt 2-6-0s and Black Fives arrived plus one B1 4-6-0 which represented the 'home' side. A couple of Brush Type 2s with DMUs worked all the ordinary, timetabled locals. Engines ran around their trains, pushed them into the station sidings or onto the old, truncated Louth lines and only then went to be serviced and turned on the distant turntable. Apparently the Black Fives were too big for this so they shot off to Firsby to use the triangle, although we didn't know this at the time. There was certainly water available from a small water tower and most probably, coal too,

though the servicing area was quite far away from our vantage point.

After lunch everything was reversed as trains returned to their home stations. These were detailed on a big blackboard at the station entrance with platform staff making sure that nobody was sent to the wrong destination. Long queues formed in the station forecourt and snaked away down the High Street. Families with lots of luggage; trolleys and barrows everywhere. Tickets were scrupulously checked with the station master carefully watching over his troops. This tide of trains going out began about noon and ended in mid-afternoon. We didn't see any goods trains as these had already been withdrawn from the branch; the yard was empty of anything but carriages – not one single coal wagon anywhere. Throughout the proceedings one of the porters kept telling us what was happening next as we had no timetable, apart from those down on the station noticeboards. They were quite tolerant of the two spotters and were obviously quite used to having an audience."

SOME ODDITIES

I'd never seen somersault signals before but there was one on a concrete and steel lattice post just at the end of the station loop where the single line to Sutton-on-Sea began. It had stop arms facing in both directions, also something new. There were several others dotted around. I wondered if the signal by the loop was latticed to aid resistance to the gales which frequently blew in from the sea? The line to Sutton appeared to disappear into a sea of caravans across the fields. Although not a large station by any means Mablethorpe had a large W.H. Smith bookstall and out at the perimeter of the forecourt was a hut similarly labelled and full of bicycles for, I assume, delivering newspapers around the town. The level crossing over High Street always had a member of staff present to open and close the gates across the busy road – they were controlled by a tiny lever frame directly under the footbridge which had its own little sentry box for staff on gate duty. No doubt this frame was interlocked with the distant signal box. I was used to level crossings on the NER Hornsea branch where gates were controlled by big wheels in signal boxes, so this was all very novel!

Above: A GNR cautionary sign for unwary passengers also positioned at the south end of Mablethorpe station under the footbridge. *Photo: Alec Swain © Transport Treasury*

Below: The functional but attractive timber Sutton-on-Sea station as seen on 27th September 1958 complete with swan-necked platform lamp standards and other GNR embellishments. The view of the apparently deserted station is taken from the Down platform looking south-east towards the goods yard connection on the Up line. The two long and two short sidings ran back to the goods shed behind the station buildings on the Up platform and also served Parsons the local fuel specialists. On the right is the timber waiting room beyond which was the 16-lever signal box.
Photo: © Transport Treasury

Above: The GNR Home somersault signal at the south end of platform 2 at Mablethorpe station is seen in the 'off' position for a departure on 24th April 1965. The arm is mounted on a GNR 'pear' slotted concrete post – a variation of the steel lattice or square wooden post types also surviving in use throughout Lincolnshire at this date. *Photo: Alec Swain © Transport Treasury*

On 25th August 1949 ex-GNR Ivatt D3 4-4-0 No. 2132 leaves Sutton-on-Sea with a northbound service for Mablethorpe and Louth. The carriage stock appears to be quad-art conversions of ex-GNR 6-wheel vehicles and are typical examples of the vintage stock used on the Loop until replaced by the arrival of the DMUs. Along with the very similar Ivatt D2 4-4-0s, the loco was one of the class which spent many years at Louth shed and by this date was the only remaining example still working on the local services and one of just three survivors still at work elsewhere. Completed at Doncaster during May 1898, the old veteran still looks game but although receiving its 1946 number was destined never to receive its BR equivalent (No. 62132) with withdrawal occurring during December 1950 after a brief move to Boston shed (40F) the previous month. *Photo: Courtesy RailOnline*

A 1950 timetable extract from Bradshaw's Guide.

Miles		Week Days only								
		a.m.	a.m.	a.m.	p.m.	p.m.	p.m.	p.m.	p.m. E	p.m. S
	Willoughby......dep	7 52	8 50	11 5		5 0	5 15	7 20	8 10	8 10
3	Mumby Road.........		8 56	1110		5 6	5 21		Dd	Dd
7	Sutton-on-Sea {arr	8 3	9 3	1117		5 13	5 28	7 31	8 23	8 23
	{dep	8 5	9 4	1120	2 33	5 16	5 31	7 33	8 24	8 24
9¾	Mablethorpe {arr	8 10	9 9	1125	2 38	5 21	5 36	7 38	8 29	8 29
	{dep	8 15	9 9	1129	2 40	5 25		7 40	8 32	8 32
12¾	Theddlethorpe......	8 21		1135		5 31		Cc	8 38	8 38
14¾	Saltfleetby........	8 26		1140		5 36			Zz	8 43
18½	Grimoldby..........	8 35		1149	2 56	5 45			8 52	8 52
22¾	Louth..........arr	8 44		1158	3 5	5 54		8 6	9 1	9 1

Miles		Week Days only						
		a.m.	a.m.	a.m.	a.m.	p.m.	p.m.	p.m.
	Louth..............dep	6 45	7 44		9 50	1 49	3 15	6 20
4½	Grimoldby.............		7 53		9 59	1 59	3 24	6 29
8	Saltfleetby...........		8 1		10 7	2 6	3 32	6 37
10	Theddlethorpe........		8 6		10 12	2 11	3 37	6 42
13	Mablethorpe {arr	7 8	8 12		10 18	2 17	3 43	6 48
	{dep	7 10	8 16	9 25	10 22	2 19	3 47	7 40
15¾	Sutton-on-Sea {arr	7 15	8 21	9 30	10 27	2 24	3 52	Cc
	{dep	7 16	8 22	9 33	10 28		3 55	
19¾	Mumby Road.........		8 30	9 41	10 36		4 4	
22¾	Willoughby......arr	7 28	8 36	9 47	10 42		4 10	8 6

In this late GNR-era view of day trippers arriving at Mablethorpe, straw boaters, summer dresses and floral hats are much in evidence, but ties are still de rigueur for the gentlemen irrespective of the weather. Two ticket inspectors man the temporary barrier as the crowd pass through ready to partake of the bracing East Coast air. The view looks north from the footbridge and just visible to the left and beyond the goods shed is a glimpse of Mablethorpe engine shed with its unique windmill for pumping water.
Photo: Courtesy Lens of Sutton Association

In the Summer of 1964, a long queue of holiday makers throng Mablethorpe High Street whilst waiting to board trains taking them home – proof that dependence on rail to reach holiday destinations was still essential for many and would continue to be so despite the findings of the Beeching Report a year earlier. From one of the recently arrived trains other visitors head in the opposite direction to find their holiday accommodation. View looking east taken from the station footbridge.
Photo: F. J. Soar/A. J. Ludlam collection

A close-up view of the main station building at Mumby Road during the last week of operations in October 1970. By this date the large timber goods shed located behind the station building had been demolished, the sidings lifted and now with only the passing loop serving the platform.
Photo: Howe Collection

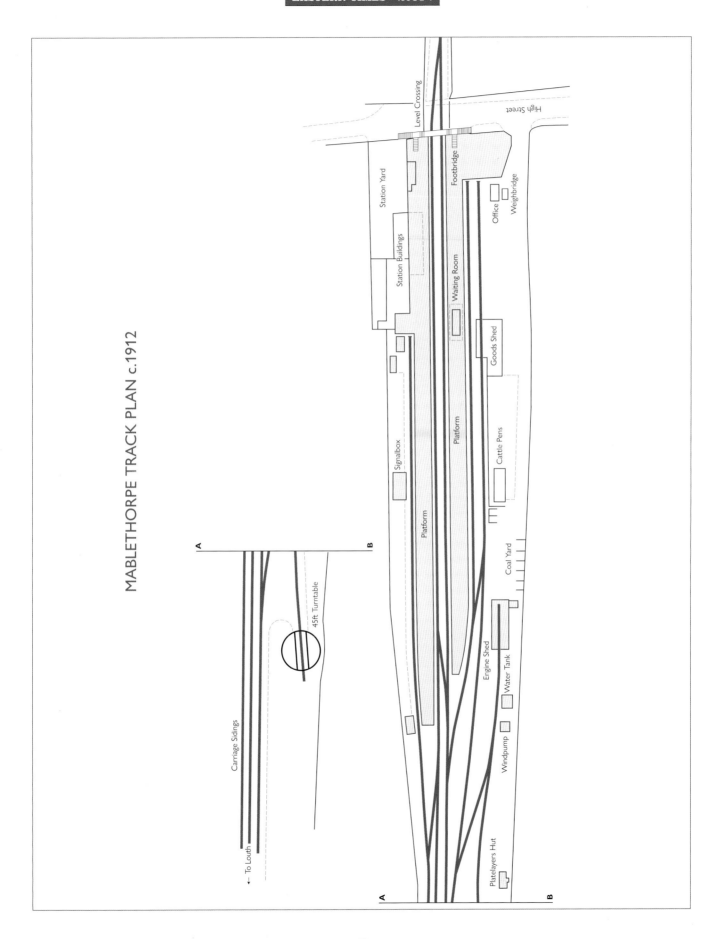

MABLETHORPE TRACK PLAN c.1912

Carriage Sidings

To Louth

45ft Turntable

A

B

Signalbox

Platform

Platform

Station Yard

Station Buildings

Waiting Room

Office

Weighbridge

Footbridge

Level Crossing

High Street

Goods Shed

Cattle Pens

Coal Yard

Engine Shed

Water Tank

Windpump

Platelayers Hut

A

B

An undated view of B1 4-6-0 No. 61302 (from 35A New England shed) entering the Down platform at Willoughby station from the south. The second carriage is an inspection saloon and the train is about to take the Mablethorpe loop, indicated by the signalman on the platform holding the tablet for the branch. The attractive 50-lever signal box had opened in 1886 in conjunction with the opening of the S&WR and the re-siting of the station to the north side of Station Road. As with many other stations in the area, the careful tending of the platform floral displays is obviously something that the station staff took great pride in which was rewarded with regular 'Best Kept Station' awards with the proving certificates displayed in the waiting room. The first was won in 1924 and afterwards the station won eight 'First' and seven 'Special' awards. With cruel irony, the station won its last award the year before its closure in October 1970. *Photo: Neville Stead © Transport Treasury*

Looking north from the footbridge in Station Road, during 1964 a Derby 2-car DMU including E56048 arrives at Willoughby station with a service to Peterborough. The train incorporates a 'tail load' in the shape of an ex-Southern Railway parcels van. Over in the Mablethorpe bay another Derby DMU waits with a northbound connecting service for the Mablethorpe branch. *Photo: Courtesy RailOnline*

SOURCES CONSULTED:

Great Northern Engine Sheds Vol. 2 by Roger Griffiths and John Hooper. Challenger Books 1996.

The East Lincolnshire Railway by A.J. Ludlam. Oakwood Press 1991.

The Louth, Mablethorpe and Willoughby Loop by A.J. Ludlam. Oakwood Press 1987.

Railways of Lincolnshire by Paul Anderson. Irwell Press 1992.

The Great Northern Railway Vols 1-3 by John Wrottesley. Batsford 1979-81.

The RCTS Locomotives of the LNER 'Green Guide'. Various volumes.

Disused Stations website.

Six Bells Junction Railtour Files.

Various editions of The Railway Observer.

With particular thanks to Richard Morton for his memory of Mablethorpe in 1964, Nick Fleetwood for signalling info and Dave Enefer, photo archivist for the Lincolnshire Coast Light Railway.

WHAT THE RAILWAYS DID FOR US

BY PAUL KING

One's perception of a place depends very much on whether you have knowledge of the area. If you have never visited one may assume that Yorkshire is all dark satanic mills, coal mines and wild and windy moors or Scotland is all lochs and glens with everyone wearing kilts. So too with Lincolnshire, it is portrayed as a rural, virtually flat county, devoted to agriculture. Certainly, much of the county is low lying, particularly in the fenland areas to the south.

However, further north there are two ridges running south from the banks of the Humber Estuary. In the west, bordering the east bank of the River Trent, is the Lincoln Edge extending south through the county to its southern border at Stamford. There is one distinct break at Lincoln, known as the Lincoln Gap, where the River Witham has cut through. The Lincoln Edge is a limestone ridge with the town of Scunthorpe located towards the northern end. To the east are the Lincolnshire Wolds, a southerly extension of the Yorkshire Wolds, separated from the Edge by the Lincoln Vale, carved out many years ago by the rivers Ancholme flowing north and Witham flowing

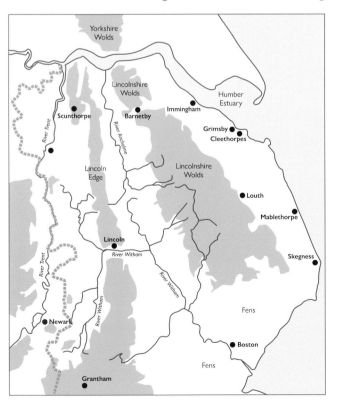

south. The Wolds are a range of rolling hills which end abruptly at Partney just to the north of Boston. Again, there is one distinct break in the Wolds at Barnetby, the Barnetby Gap. Beyond the Wolds to the east is an area of relatively low-lying fertile marshland effectively cut off from the rest of the county by these two ranges of hills and the Lincolnshire Fens to the south.

The area to the east of the Wolds is relatively unknown to many people as it is not an area you pass through; it is an area you go to. The North Sea and the Humber Estuary are effective barriers to onward travel. Lincoln and Grantham are well known for their engineering and Scunthorpe for steel, but it is this fertile coastal belt to the east of the Wolds that is the most heavily industrialised with the petro-chemical industry stretching along the south bank of the Humber from Immingham to Grimsby. Grimsby, once the world's premier fishing port is now seeing its success grow again through a burgeoning renewable energy support network. Immingham, now the largest bulk handling port in the U.K., is around 5 miles north-west of Grimsby whilst the resort of Cleethorpes is separated by the width of a road with the two towns having no discernible border. Fourteen miles south of Grimsby is the market town of Louth, the largest town in this north-eastern part of Lincolnshire for many years. Mablethorpe is on the east coast 15 miles from Louth with Skegness a further 15 miles to the south.

Grimsby, or to give it its full title, Great Grimsby, is the fourth oldest County Borough in England with its first charter dating from 1201, four years before Lincoln received its first charter. Immingham is now a small town but for many years was little more than a small village with its main claim to fame being that the Pilgrim Fathers sheltered there in 1608 before fleeing to Holland to start a new life.

The positions of Immingham, Grimsby and Cleethorpes on the south bank of the Humber Estuary show how remote they were from the rest of the county. The gap through the Lincoln Edge at Lincoln and the Lincolnshire Wolds at Barnetby can be clearly seen as can the barrier of the fens to the south. When iron ore deposits were discovered in the Scunthorpe area the railways could no longer use the low lying contours of the land and substantial embankments and inclines were needed to access these deposits.

The south end of Louth station on 3rd July 1936. New England Class C1 No. 4403 waits in platform 3 with a semi-fast for Peterborough, whilst Class D2 No. 4397 is in the bay platform with a train for Mablethorpe. I had the impression that Immingham had an allocation of the Ivatt Atlantics, as they were a common sight around Grimsby, but none were ever on the books and New England locomotives covered the prestige East Lincs services. *Photo: H. C. Casserley – Paul King Collection*

Cleethorpes is the result of the amalgamation of three of the five hamlets that formed the Thorpe of Clee. The actual date that Oole, Itterby and Thrunscoe became Cleethorpes is unclear but by 1800 the area was being referred to by that name. Incidentally, the other two Thorpes of Clee, Weelsby and Clee, are now within the boundaries of Great Grimsby. It is these three towns in the northern part of the area on which this article will concentrate.

The fortunes of all three towns have risen and fallen over the years and by the 1830s they were possibly at their lowest. Within 20 years Grimsby's fortunes would change dramatically as it prospered and grew. Cleethorpes had to wait a further 10 years before development would bring success. It would be into the 20th century before Immingham experienced the same benefits. Why? Quite simply, investment by railway companies. The current towns of Great Grimsby, Cleethorpes and Immingham are, effectively, railway towns as without the foresight of the railway companies, specifically the Manchester, Sheffield and Lincolnshire Railway, there is a possibility that these towns would have ceased to exist.

Railways were already well established by the time eyes were being cast towards Lincolnshire's east coast. In total three separate Acts of Parliament were required for the Great Grimsby & Sheffield Junction Railway (GG&SJR) – 30th June 1845, East Lincolnshire Railway (ELR) – 26th June 1846 and the Sheffield & Lincolnshire Junction

Railway (S&LJR) – 3rd August 1846. Also, on the 27th July 1846, an act authorising the amalgamation of the GG&SJR and the S&LJR into the Manchester, Sheffield and Lincolnshire Railway (MS&LR), along with the Manchester, Ashton-under-Lyne and Sheffield Junction Railway, was passed which took effect from the 1st January 1847. All of these acts were passed as the 'Railway Mania' reached its peak. Many fanciful proposals collapsed and many early pioneers disappeared, ignominiously, from the scene. Fortunately, for the future of North-Eastern Lincolnshire, all of these schemes went ahead.

The East Lincolnshire Railway proposed a line running north from Boston along the eastern edge of the Wolds to Louth and on to Grimsby. At Boston it would form a junction with the Great Northern Railway, whose plans were to build a railway from London northwards. The ELR, although nominally independent until the grouping in 1923, was always operated by the Great Northern Railway (GNR) although that company's trains didn't reach Boston until the 17th October 1848, 15 days after those of the ELR.

The GG&SJR and the S&LJR planned a line west from Sheffield via Worksop, Retford, Gainsborough and Brigg to Grimsby and New Holland on the Humber. Also included was a branch line from Brigg to Market Rasen and Lincoln, this line eventually took an easier route leaving the main line at Wrawby, just to the west of Barnetby.

Ex-GCR Class 8F, LNER Class B4 4-6-0 No. 1482 *Immingham* became something of a celebrity when it was repainted into LNER green. It is seen at Barnetby in the early months of 1947 whilst based at Lincoln working a stopping train from Cleethorpes to its home city. Transferred to Ardsley in July 1947, this loco became the last ex-GCR 4-6-0 to be withdrawn when it was condemned in November 1950, it never received its BR number. *Photo: Neville Stead Collection © Transport Treasury*

The Royal Dock in the 1920s before the old coal jetties extending onto the dock were swept away and replaced by a single jetty with coaling towers. Dominating the dock is the hydraulic tower built on the island between the two sets of lock gates, 309ft high it provided power, not only for operating the lock gates, but to many more of the ports facilities. Known to generations of 'Grimbarians' as the Dock Tower it is the first thing we look for when returning home. The Italianate design is based on the *Torre Del Mangia* in Sienna and is the only Grade 1 listed building in the area other than churches. *Photo: Dave Cowell Collection*

Construction commenced in 1847 and on the 1st March 1848 the New Holland to Grimsby section of the MS&LR and the Louth to Grimsby section of the ELR opened with a joint service from Louth to New Holland. The ELR extended its operations south to Firsby on the 3rd September 1848 and on to Boston a month later on the 2nd October. On the MS&LR the section from Ulceby to Brigg and from Wrawby to Market Rasen opened on the 1st November 1848. The extension from Market Rasen to Lincoln being brought into use on the 1st December. A branch from New Holland to Barton-upon-Humber opened on the 1st March 1849 followed by the Brigg-Gainsborough section on the 2nd April. The final section, from Gainsborough to Woodhouse Junction (Sheffield), came into public use from the 17th July 1849. At Lincoln all the railways, the Great Northern and the Midland Railway, which also had lines running into the city, were funnelled through the Lincoln Gap. Further north the only access to the coastal belt, avoiding expensive cuttings and tunnelling, was through the Barnetby Gap. Moving on a few years from the opening, three lines joined at Wrawby Junction, the Lincoln Branch, the Main Line, from Gainsborough and the Yorkshire Branch running in from Doncaster via Thorne and Scunthorpe. Once through the Gap the line divided at Brocklesby with one line heading north to New Holland and the other east towards Grimsby.

The Hull & Selby Railway (later to be part of the North Eastern Railway) had, by 1845, effectively closed off the port of Hull from incursion by other railways, although the Hull & Barnsley Railway did make inroads from 1885. The MS&LR extension to New Holland was classed as the main line until 1883 with passengers for Grimsby initially changing at Ulceby. This practice had ceased long before the reduction in status to branch line.

Having acquired the ferry services across the Humber in 1845, the MS&LR constructed a pier at New Holland extending 1,500ft into the Humber so that services could arrive and depart at any time of day, the Humber is tidal and a floating pontoon was required in order to achieve this. Suitable for passengers and light goods, this service didn't achieve the goal of access to the port of Hull for heavy goods. For this, the MS&LR turned east to Grimsby where there were port facilities, of a limited nature. Grimsby had a connection with the sea from its inception around the 8th century although access was via a creek that tended to silt up depending on the tidal flow in the Humber. Late in the 18th century the Grimsby Haven Co. attempted to develop the port facilities with a dock close to the centre of the town, unfortunately it relied on the, aforementioned, creek and by the late 1830s the port was, virtually, derelict. The Grimsby Haven Co. became part of the GG&SJR in 1845 and, therefore, part of the MS&LR.

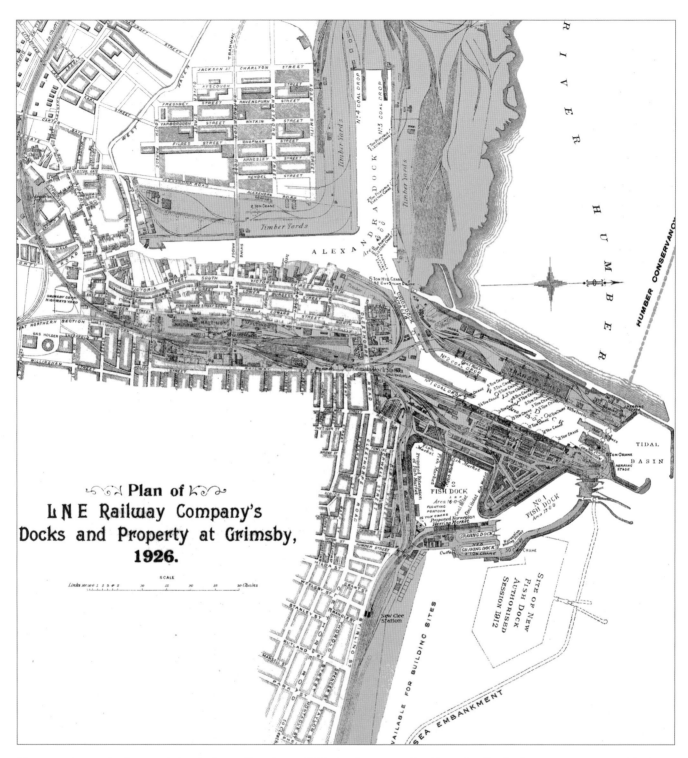

Plan of
LNE Railway Company's
Docks and Property at Grimsby,
1926.

This map shows the layout of the docks at Grimsby in 1926. At the top is the Alexandra Dock showing as a reversed L shape. The bottom half of this dock, extending south towards the centre of the town, is the Old Dock and the creek which originally served it is running north along the west side the Royal Dock. The narrow Union dock is in the centre of the map connecting the Royal and Alexandra docks. The two coal drops at the south end of the Royal Dock were about to be replaced by a new quay, on the site of the western, No.2 Coal Drop, with enhanced coal loading facilities, whilst the two coal drops at the western end of the Alexandra Dock would soon fall out of use. To the east, or below, the Royal Dock are Fish docks Nos.1 and 2. No.1 is on the site of the original Fish Craft Dock although much enlarged. To the east of No.1 Fish dock is the site of the new fish dock authorised in 1912. This would eventually be constructed by the LNER and opened in 1934. It became known, appropriately, as No.3 Fish Dock.

The proposal was to build a new dock into the estuary from a point adjacent to and east of the lock gates for the original dock. The plan called for a dock extending ¾ mile out from the shoreline and reclaiming 138 acres of land. The enclosed dock would cover 20 acres with a further 13 acres in a tidal basin. Access was to be by two locks, both 300 feet long, with one being 70 feet wide and the other 40 feet. This meant that the new dock could accept the largest ships of the day. The foundation stone for the new dock was laid by Prince Albert on the 18th April 1849 and the dock was brought into use on the 27th May 1852. It was officially opened by Queen Victoria on the 14th October 1854, in honour of her visit the dock became known as the Royal Dock.

Fishing, as with any coastal town, was a staple part of life but until the arrival of the railways there was a very limited market with the catch rarely being sold much further away than Lincoln and the Lincolnshire market towns. It was noticeable that there were an increasing number of fishing vessels landing their catches at the port. Railway connection had opened new markets and both the MS&LR and the GNR, through their involvement with the East Lincs line, saw the potential for developing trade. The MS&LR formed the Deep Sea Fishing Co. in 1854, they were soon joined by the GNR and the Midland Railway, which hoped to pick up a percentage of the trade via Lincoln, to operate fishing vessels and to attract fishing vessel owners from other parts of the country. To handle the expected trade a 6-acre Fishing Craft Dock with a floating pontoon for unloading the catches was built to the east of the Royal Dock. The floating pontoon soon fell out of use as the fishing trade expanded but its name lives on. The Grimsby fish market, in its prime, was over a mile long and was universally known as the pontoon and even today it is commemorated at Blundell Park, the home of Grimsby Town F.C., where the home fans congregate in the Pontoon Stand.

The stagnating and dying town of Grimsby had a population of just 3,700 in 1841. By 1851 vibrancy, prosperity and hope had been restored with the population more than doubling to just under 9,000, by the end of the century this had risen to 75,000. This was all due to the foresight of the investors that promoted the GG&SJR and ELR and the continued investment that came with the growth. The name Grimsby became synonymous with fish, from the small 6-acre dock of 1854 the facilities gradually expanded during the 1860s with the widening and extending of the original dock. In 1876 construction began on a second fish dock, covering 11 acres, immediately to the south of the original fish dock and accessed through that dock. This dock, known as No.2 Fish Dock, the original becoming No.1, was extended by a further 5 acres in 1894 causing the Cleethorpes branch (qv) to be realigned with the tortuous reverse curves that exist to this day. Capacity was still at a premium and it was said you could walk across the dock on the decks of trawlers when the fleet was in port. Despite many proposals by the Great Central Railway (GCR), the 1897 successor to the MS&LR, it would be 1934 before this was addressed when a third dock, covering 38 acres and appropriately named No. 3 Fish Dock, was constructed to the east of No. 1 Fish Dock.

The commercial dock too was going from strength to strength. In 1853 just over 500 vessels carrying 134,000 tons passed through the port, 10 years later there were almost 1,400 recorded with a tonnage handled approaching 320,000. The most significant difference was in the amount of coal handled for export, this had risen from zero in 1853 to 170,000 tons in 1863. The major import at this time was Scandinavian timber and this amounted to 120,000 tons. A passenger and cargo service to Hamburg was inaugurated as soon as the dock opened. This service had doubled by 1855 and further services to other northern European ports had been introduced. The MS&LR was working hard and its enterprise and vision were paying off. In 1856 in conjunction with the South Yorkshire Railway and some French interests, the MS&LR promoted the Anglo-French Steamship Co. with the intention of exporting coal to France. This was the acorn from which the MS&LR built its continental fleet of steamships, all based at Grimsby. Incidentally, the South Yorkshire Railway became part of the MS&LR in 1864.

Demand was outstripping capacity and in 1873 a new dock, linking the Royal Dock with the Old Dock, still served by locks opening onto the old creek, was authorised. To be called the Union Dock, also referred to as a canal, it was 870ft long with a width of 100ft. The entrance lock, from the Royal Dock was 340ft long and 45ft wide. The Union dock was opened in 1879. Capacity was still at a premium and several proposals were put forward. The one chosen was for a 26-acre extension of the Old Dock that would run at right angles to it at the northern end together with extensive improvements to the Old Dock. The Old Dock improvements and the new extension were brought into use during 1880 and the whole was renamed the Alexandra Dock in honour of Princess Alexandra who accompanied her husband, the Prince of Wales, at the opening of the Union Dock. This completes the investment in the port of Grimsby, all instigated by the MS&LR and its successors.

The MS&LR wasn't just the creator of the port of Grimsby, it was also developing, a couple of miles to the east, a holiday resort, Cleethorpes. From the early 1800s onwards Cleethorpes was attracting visitors who came to take the sea air. The potential that could be realised with the arrival of the railway wasn't lost on its residents nor was it lost on the MS&LR. A branch line to Cleethorpes had been authorised at the same time as the other lines in the area but it would take until 1863 before this was achieved. Protracted discussions with landowners about the route the line was to take over the East Marsh of Grimsby delayed progress until agreement was finally reached and a single-track branch opened on the 6th April 1863. Ironically, the route taken was virtually identical to the MS&LR's original proposal of 1849. It was certainly needed. Excursion trains were arriving at Grimsby Town and Grimsby Docks station where holidaymakers would alight and make their way via Cleethorpe Road to the seaside, often behind marching bands. Note the spelling of Cleethorpe Road, it is the road to the Thorpe of Clee, not the road to Cleethorpes, hence no 's' on the end of the name. Having reached Cleethorpes, it was now incumbent on the railway company to provide facilities for the visitors it brought to the town.

The single-track branch line to Cleethorpes soon proved insufficient and by 1874 the line had been doubled. In 1880 the station was extended from two to six platforms. Often at a seaside resort the station is in the town, remote from the beach, one only needs to look at Scarborough, Bridlington, Skegness, Blackpool (after the closure of Central), or Bournemouth. Not so at Cleethorpes, the only obstacle between the station and the beach is the north promenade. The platforms and tracks were often covered in wind-blown sand. As noted in the previous paragraph, to attract visitors you need attractions. The MS&LR were approached and asked if they would undertake works for the protection and preservation of the coastline. In 1882 they purchased 17 acres of land and from 1883 the development of Cleethorpes as a resort began in earnest. A pier had been built as long ago as 1872 by a private

Cleethorpes station in the summer of 1937. The original platforms, 1 and 2, are to the right with the 1880 additions, platforms 3-6 centre and left. To the rear can be seen the clock tower, built at the same time the station was extended and recently restored to its former glory. The 4-4-0, No. 5684, sits in platform 4 with a stopping train for New Holland, whilst in platform 3 one of the compound Atlantics, No. 5364 *Lady Faringdon*, has charge of a stopping service although the coaches appear to have roof boards. 5684 was in the twilight of its career, being withdrawn in June 1939 after spending the whole of its LNER career allocated to sheds in the area, Immingham, New Holland and Louth. The C5 Atlantics came to Immingham in the mid-1930s and made it their home for the rest of their lives. 5364 was the loco that hauled the Royal Train at the opening of Immingham Dock in 1912, it was withdrawn in 1946 as LNER No. 2897. *Photo: Neville Stead Collection © Transport Treasury*

The beach and promenade at Cleethorpes, shortly after World War 1. Holidaymakers, almost all day trippers arriving by train, leave barely a patch of sand free whilst hundreds more throng the promenade. To the left are the clock tower and refreshment rooms at Cleethorpes station. The Sea Wall, clock tower and refreshments are all that survive today, all the beachside amusements have long since disappeared.
Photo: Edward Trevitt, courtesy Wendy Trevitt

company which was associated with the MS&LR. Extending 1,200ft into the Humber Estuary. The length meant that at all states of the tide part of the pier was in the water, the tidal flow at Cleethorpes and the flat nature of the bed of the estuary means that the high and low water marks are a considerable distance apart. In 1884 the pier was officially acquired by the MS&LR who built a pavilion at the seaward end In 1888. Fire overtook the structure in 1903 and considerable damage resulted. Both the pier and pavilion were repaired and an additional pavilion built closer inshore with a raised entranceway crossing the promenade. This opened in 1905. The raised entrance was demolished shortly before World War II and the pier itself breached against invasion shortly after the start of the war. This breach was never repaired and the 900 feet between the new pavilion and the end of the pier were demolished after the war. The new pavilion survives and is currently owned by a national fish and chip chain.

Prior to the acquisition of the pier, work had begun on a defensive sea wall and this progressed over the next few years until swimming baths, a restaurant, colonnade and refreshment rooms were built. Gardens were landscaped and the promenade provided with lighting, something relatively unique at the time. Later in the century a grotto was constructed in the cliff gardens. The initial developments were officially opened by Prince Albert Victor on the 2nd July 1885. In 1891 further extensions were made to the sea wall and a further 33 acres of land acquired by the MS&LR. The company now owned the entire coastline from High Cliff in Cleethorpes to Pyewipe,

west of Grimsby. Amongst the foreshore developments undertaken during 1885 was the construction of a folly at High Cliff. Known as Ross Castle, it is a mock ruin of a castle and is named after the then secretary of the MS&LR, Edward Ross.

To summarise the work of the MS&LR in developing both Grimsby and Cleethorpes there is little better than these quotes from the Great Central Railway's Official Album. The MS&LR was renamed the Great Central Railway in 1897 after completion of its London extension.

Grimsby was described thus, from a series of articles on ports of the U.K. by 'the Mariner'. *"The Manchester, Sheffield and Lincolnshire Railway found Grimsby in the depths of despair, and they have raised it up to a high pitch of exultancy at things achieved and of hope for things to be achieved in the future. Nor is this any great wonder. Connecting Grimsby directly with the salt mines of Cheshire and the richest coal districts of South Yorkshire, the railway company, from these sources alone, has sufficient store to foster any port that they might choose to open; and when it is remembered that Grimsby is undoubtedly the port above all others adapted for the trade between the Midlands and Eastern parts of England and the Northern ports of Europe, it will readily be understood how, with a powerful company , well furnished with the sinews of trade to back it, it has at length recovered all of and more of its ancient prosperity. But besides the two great sources of wealth referred to above, the Manchester, Sheffield and Lincolnshire Railway Co.*

A superb aerial view of the Grimsby Dock from the east, the coaling jetties with their towers are in the middle of the photograph. The North Wall on the right curves away to the lock gates. South Quay with the Refitting Quays and slipways are on the left with No. 2 Fish Dock above them. The Pontoon, fish market, can be seen running along the length of both No. 1 and No. 2 Fish docks and was almost a mile in length. *Photo: Eric Green*

are in touch with all the principal manufacturing towns of the central belt of the United Kingdom: Barrow, Birmingham, Derby, Doncaster, Halifax, Huddersfield, Leeds, Liverpool, Manchester, Nottingham, Peterborough, Sheffield, Wakefield, Warrington, all avail themselves of the facilities for the shortest transit to the Baltic and North Sea ports; nor does London itself disdain to look upon Grimsby as a useful outlet for its merchandise; while to all the great towns and the capital itself, Grimsby, as a feeder from foreign ports, is invaluable."

Cleethorpes was described thus. *"Beyond Grimsby the line has been pushed to Cleethorpes, a village once inhabited by a few fishermen only in winter, but now changed by a unique effort of railway enterprise into the most crowded watering place in Lincolnshire. It is almost entirely the property of the Great Central Railway, who have built there a massive sea wall, 65 feet wide, the inner side of which is a broad carriage drive, divided from the promenade by a dwarf wall. A pier, a switch-back, public gardens, and other places of amusements, have been built by the enterprise of the company, and in summer the town is thronged with excursionists from Yorkshire, Lancashire and the Midlands."*

Written in the idiom of the turn of the century, one, nevertheless, understands the pride taken by the company in its achievements. The importance of Cleethorpes to the MS&LR can be gleaned from an incident at Whitsun 1888. Smallpox had broken out in Grimsby with some cases being reported as close to the resort as New Clee, barely a mile from the terminus. Initially, the company cancelled all

trains but a public outcry caused them to be reinstated on the understanding they ran non-stop through Grimsby and New Clee. The total investment by the company in Cleethorpes was in the region of £100,000, approximately £12million today, but visitors came in their thousands, 30,000 a day was not unknown. An investment repaid time and time again.

The driving force behind many of the developments was the general manager of the MS&LR from 1854 to 1861 and its enigmatic chairman from 1864 to 1894, Edward Watkin. He died in 1901 but his influence could still be seen in the next major development in the area, Immingham Dock.

The official party at the turning of the sod ceremony for Immingham Dock on 12th July 1906. As far as I can identify, on the front row from the left are the Bishop of Lincoln, Sir Alexander Henderson, Lady Henderson, unidentified, Sir William Pollitt, Sir George Doughty M.P., Mrs Harry Pollitt, Sam Fay, Mrs Fay, Lady Pollitt and two of Sam Fay's daughters. The ceremony was performed by Lady Henderson.
Photo: Immingham Museum Collection

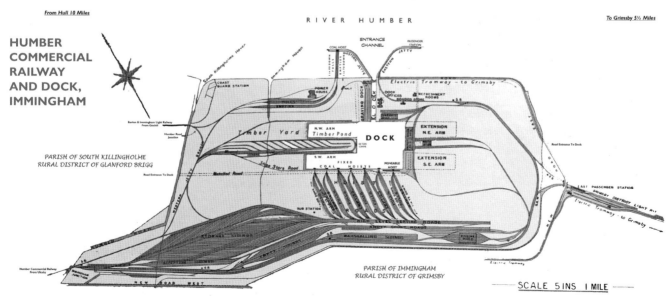

Great Central Compound Atlantic Class 8E 4-4-2 No. 364 *Lady Henderson* was selected to head the Royal Train. It is seen here, suitably adorned, awaiting departure with the King and Queen. *Lady Henderson* would work the train to Grimsby where a Great Northern engine would take over. Renamed *Lady Faringdon*, when Lord Henderson was raised to the peerage in 1917, this loco came to Immingham in the 1930s where it worked out its career on passenger trains from Cleethorpes. *Photo: Immingham Museum Collection*

When further expansion of the docks at Grimsby was required in the early 1870s the MS&LR instructed its Consulting Engineer, Charles Liddell, to survey possible sites. His report, submitted in the spring of 1874, favoured a site to the west of Grimsby at Killingholme. Here the deep-water channel was a mere 300 yards offshore whereas at Grimsby the distance was more than 1,500 yards, which required regular dredging. The proposal was shelved when the improvements were made at Grimsby. However, there is no doubt that a new dock further west was still on the cards and plans would have been formulating in the offices of the MS&LR towards the end of Watkin's career. During 1900 the need for additional facilities were again becoming urgent and negotiations between the GCR and Grimsby Corporation resulted in a new dock being built, not on the western border of Grimsby but 5 miles upstream at Immingham. Work commenced in 1906 and the dock was formally opened on 22nd July 1912. The first ship to use the new facility, in 1910, albeit at a jetty in the estuary was, appropriately, one of the GCR's own ships, the S.S. Dewsbury.

The MS&LR had always been bold with their developments and so was its successor, endorsing the word on its coat of arms, 'Forward'. The plans for the new dock called for an enclosed dock space of 45 acres on a dock estate of almost 1,000 acres. At its closest point, Little London level crossing near Stallingborough, the new dock was just under 2½ miles away from the nearest railway line. The act for the construction of the new dock was passed on the 22nd July 1904 and authorised not only the construction of the dock but three railways to connect it with the national system.

To say the scheme was ambitious is an understatement, the speculation was based on the adage 'Build it and trade will come.' Additionally the land was extremely low lying and marshy and would require raising by at least 5 feet. This was achieved by using the material excavated from the dock and from the mud pumped ashore from the excavation of the deep water channel.

The dock was designed on a north-west to south-east alignment alongside the estuary. As built the dock was a U-shape laid on its side; although there was potential to increase capacity at the south-eastern end by transforming the dock into an H-shape, these extensions were never built. Access from the estuary was via a lock 840ft in length and 90ft wide and was designed to be accessible at

Looking towards the dock from the high-level lines showing Nos. 4 to 7 coal hoists. On the left are the lines for loaded coal leading to the concrete bridges in the distance for Nos. 5 and 6 hoists and on the right are return lines for empty wagons. The power-house, built to provide power to the dock estate, can be seen in the distance. *Photo: Immingham Museum Collection*

all states of the tide. The entrance was protected by two jetties extending 650ft into the Humber. The Western Jetty was intended for bunkering ships with coal, this was the jetty used by the Dewsbury in 1910. The Eastern Jetty was designed as a passenger terminal and there were fanciful designs for station buildings on the jetty that were never built.

The cutting of the first sod ceremony took place on the 12th July 1906 with the official opening ceremony taking place 6 years and 10 days later. In the intervening years the contractors, Price, Wills & Reeve, employed over 3,000 workers, more than 30 locomotives, 10 steam navvies and more than 1,500 wagons in the construction. Along the 2,350 ft. south quay, seven coal hoists were constructed all supplied by high level service lines from a large group of sidings to the west known as Reception Sidings, shown as Storage Sidings on the attached plan. Wagons returned by gravity to low level shunt sidings from where they were transferred to the, appropriately named, Empty Sidings. The quay extending into the dock from the north-west handled minerals on the south side and timber on the north side. Adjacent to the lock was a graving dock 740 feet in length. South-east of the lock was No. 1 Transit Quay and this was connected to the South Quay by Nos. 2 and 3 transit quays. Dominant along these latter quays was the grain warehouse, seven storeys and over

100 feet in height. Referred to as Fay's Folly, Sam Fay was the General Manager of the GCR at the time, the port struggled to find trade initially and was taken over by the Royal Navy during World War 1. Steady growth since has seen Immingham develop into one of the major ports in the U.K. and become the largest bulk handling port in the country.

Noted earlier was the need to build new railways to the dock. The first was the Grimsby District Light Railway. This left the Barnetby-Grimsby line at Marsh Junction and included the realignment of the Grimsby Docks branch, built for the opening of the Alexandra Dock. On reaching the coast the line swung north-west towards Immingham and was never more than a few hundred yards from the shoreline. The Grimsby & Immingham Electric Railway, built to transport workers between Grimsby and Immingham, was laid alongside the southern side of this line after leaving the street section in Grimsby. The Humber Commercial Railway, by far the busiest and most important of the new lines, left the New Holland line north of Ulceby station and swung south-eastwards to enter the dock estate at Humber Road on the south-western edge of the new works. The third was the Barton & Immingham Light Railway. This left the dock estate on the north-western side and travelled via East Halton to Goxhill, on the New Holland branch. Closed in 1963, the land has not been sold off as it is seen as a potential alternative outlet from the docks although, after this length of time, I doubt that will ever happen.

Having mentioned the closure of the Barton & Immingham Light Railway, it would be appropriate to list the other closures. Compared to some parts of the country these have not been major. The East Lincolnshire Line, from Garden Street in Grimsby to Werrington Junction north of Peterborough, closed in October 1970, although the Boston to Firsby South Junction section was retained for services to Skegness and the Spalding to Werrington Junction section re-opened shortly after closure. The Grimsby & Immingham Electric Railway, the Immingham trams, closed on the 1st July 1961 and 20 years later New Holland Pier closed concurrent with the opening of the Humber Bridge. The Grimsby District Light Railway remains open although single tracked and little used, it is maintained as an alternative route should the Humber Commercial Railway be closed for any reason. The Cleethorpes branch has been singled from Garden Street to the approach to Cleethorpes station where four of the six platforms remain serviceable. I should quantify the use of the word major earlier in this paragraph, I have used it in relation

to services into the area. The effect it has had on the railway desert that is central and eastern Lincolnshire is devastating.

On the approaches to Grimsby Town there are three level crossings with a fourth on the opposite side of the station, all within less than ½ mile. People bemoan the delays caused by these crossings and complain generally about railways. Little do they realise that without these railways it is possible they would not exist as their ancestors only came to the town because of the railway so it is unlikely their grandparents or great grandparents would ever have met. Therefore, what the railways have done for us, besides creating the prosperity of the three towns, is bring people together whose descendants now live and work in that creation.

I have drawn heavily on my own series, *The Railways of North East Lincolnshire*. This has been published by myself as a pictorial and textual history of the area in five parts. If you would like to know more, please contact me by email at *goneegging@hotmail.co.uk* or telephone 07873 125247. All five parts of *The Railways of North East Lincolnshire* are available from me.

Immingham Reception Sidings shortly before World War I with a generous mix of private owner and GCR owned wagons. In the distance the coal hoists along the South Quay at Immingham Dock can be seen on the right horizon. The power station is on the centre horizon.
Photo: Paul King Collection

CAMBRIDGE IN PICTURES

1 and 2. Contrasting views of Cambridge station frontage, although two years after nationalisation the LNER signage above the unattractive awning still dominates on 29th January 1950. The second view was taken on 30th May 1966 with BR signage above the improved awning and centre bays.

3. Holden Class J69/1 0-6-0T No. E8579, pictured on station carriage duties, is sandwiched between coaches of the GWR, LMS and SR on 20th April 1949.

4. A busy Cambridge shed and loco yard as pictured in 1959, the two locos identifiable are K1 2-6-0 No. 62037 and to its left Holden Class E4 2-4-0 No. 62785.

5. A view of Cambridge Up Yard on 11th February 1949.

6. A view south from the station with Hills Road Bridge in the distance on the right.

7. Holden Class D16/3 4-4-0 No. 62543, pictured on shed at Cambridge on 19th May 1957.

8. A busy Cambridge shed pictured on 8th April 1951. Numbered 31A the shed was located to the west side of the line at the north end of the station.

9. Class D16/3 4-4-0 No. 62589 departs Cambridge on an express working and passes Class K1 2-6-0 No. 62020. The K1 was introduced in 1949 and was a Peppercorn development of Thompson's K1/1.

10. Thompson Class B2 4-6-0 No. 61671 *Royal Sovereign* awaits departure with the 3.10pm service to Kings Cross while Class B17/4 4-6-0 No. 61653 *Huddersfield Town* gets under way with the 2.55pm the Liverpool Street on 24th February 1953. On the right is Holden Class E4 2-4-0 No. 62786 on carriage pilot duties.

All images © Transport Treasury

THE HEADSHUNT

In future issues our aim is to bring you many differing articles about the LNER, its constituent companies and the Eastern and North Eastern regions of British Railways. We hope to have gone some way to achieving this in Issue 1.

Eastern Times welcomes constructive comment from readers either by way of additional information on subjects already published or suggestions for new topics that you would like to see addressed. The size and diversity of the LNER, due to it being comprised of many different companies each with their differing ways of operating, shows the complexity of the subject and we will endeavour to be as accurate as possible but would appreciate any comments to the contrary.

We want to use this final page – The Headshunt – as your platform for comment and discussion so please feel free to send your comments to: tteasterntimes@gmail.com or write to Eastern Times, Transport Treasury Publishing Ltd., 16 Highworth Close, High Wycombe HP13 7PJ.

Darlington – July 1961
An ex-works Class J27 No. 65791 hauls a line of locomotives out of the works headed by Class B16/2 No 61457, a Gresley rebuild of a Vincent Raven Class B16.